GAP YEARS

The Essential Guide

Need — 2 — Know

Emma Jayne Jones

First published in Great Britain in 2009 by
Need2Know
Remus House
Coltsfoot Drive
Peterborough
PE2 9JX
Telephone 01733 898103
Fax 01733 313524
www.need2knowbooks.co.uk

Need2Know is an imprint of Forward Press Ltd.
www.forwardpress.co.uk
All Rights Reserved
© Emma Jones 2009
SB ISBN 978-1-86144-079-2
Cover photograph: Jupiter Images

Contents

Introduction

You can read about the world in a book or watch programmes on the television, but until you get out there and grasp it with both hands, the earth might as well be flat.

There are endless places to explore, people to meet and experiences to be had, and setting off on a gap year will open up a world of opportunity and adventure.

How do you decide what to do?

Not long ago you could pretty much guarantee that a gap year would include a round-the-world flight and a stint working in Australia, but modern gap years are much more varied. There is now more emphasis on getting to know a country, taking part in volunteer work or pushing your boundaries through adventure travel. With so many options available, it can be difficult to decide which one is right for you.

Rather than bombarding you with every possible option, itinerary and detail, this book keeps it simple. Planning a gap year can be confusing enough without having things over complicated!

So, where do you start?

You may only have a few months to spare, or are planning on taking a whole year out, but either way you will want to make the most of your time away. From booking flights and planning an itinerary to choosing what to do and how to pay for it, this book will help you put the basics in place.

With helpful continent guides and chapters on volunteering and working abroad, it will give you the inspiration you need to make all those essential decisions. As well as the fun stuff, this book offers important advice on health and safety and a comprehensive help list to get your travel planning underway.

Whether you are leaving behind school, university or your career, jetting off to explore the world is an exciting and life-changing prospect. However excited you are though, it can feel a bit scary to leave behind the safety and comfort of home. While a gap year is tinged with uncertainty, that is part of the fun. If you are in doubt, listen to these wise words from Mark Twain, one of America's most famous literary icons:

'Twenty years from now you will be more disappointed by the things you didn't do than by the ones you did do. So throw off the bowlines. Sail away from the safe harbor. Catch the trade winds in your sails. Explore. Dream. Discover.'

The things you discover about yourself and the world around you on your gap year will last a lifetime. Whether it goes to plan or evolves and changes along the way, it is an adventure that you will never forget.

So get stuck in, start making some exciting decisions and get ready to have the time of your life. Happy planning!

Disclaimer

When planning a gap year, you should always consult your GP regarding the vaccinations and booster injections you will need. This guide gives a brief overview of the vaccinations you can receive, but professional medical advice is recommended.

Chapter One

Practicalities

Are you ready for a gap year?

There are plenty of reasons for taking a gap year but the main one should be because you want to. Don't decide that you 'should' take one or let your mum or best friend persuade you that it's the best thing to do. Taking a gap year requires a big investment of time and money and you only want to commit to it if you are ready and willing to do so.

You should also consider what level of support and structure you need. If you are an experienced traveller you may be happy to plan it all yourself, but if you haven't left home alone before, it may be a good idea to think about an organised programme or tour.

Choosing what to do

If you are set on taking a gap year then you need to have a clear idea of what you are going to do with it. Whether you are delaying university or your career, you need to make the most of it. The best way to make this decision is to take a thorough look at all the options. Gather brochures and books, scour websites and talk to other people who have taken a gap year to ensure that you are able to make an informed decision. There are many elements that can make up your gap year – you may decide to concentrate on one or combine them all to find the ideal mix.

'When I decided to take a gap year I had no idea where to start. Having some guidance would have been a huge help.'

Tracey, 32.

Travel

The main reason why people take a gap year is to get out and see the world. You know that once you get settled into a career, or have other commitments, it will be more difficult to take time out to travel, so this is your time to explore. You need to think carefully about where you want to go, how much you can realistically fit in and plan an itinerary.

Working abroad

Working abroad is a great way to see the world and get paid for it. It can help you get to know a country, learn a language or gain international experience for your CV. There are many options ranging from seasonal work to cruise ships, working visas or internships. These all take planning and commitment but can help combine two key aspects of a gap year – money and travel.

Working in the UK

You may have to work for a few months and save some money before you set off. Or perhaps you would rather dedicate your entire gap year to earning money or working on your career. Deciding to work for the year is admirable, but you should ask yourself how you will feel when your friends leave for university or travelling and you are left at home.

Volunteering

Volunteering abroad has soared in popularity over recent years. Volunteering allows you to give something back while getting to know the locals and immersing yourself in the culture. These programmes can be expensive, so it is worth shopping around and finding out exactly where your contribution is going.

How do you plan an itinerary?

With so much to do and see, you could spend decades travelling the world but never see it all – so how do you decide where to go? Your itinerary is going to be guided by two main considerations: what you want to do and how much money you have to do it. Start by asking yourself a few questions:

- Is there anywhere you've always wanted to go?
- What major sights would you like to see?
- What do you enjoy doing?
- How much time can you spare?
- How much time would you like to spend in each place?
- How much money do you have?

Although traditionally referred to as a 'gap year', the length of your trip may vary considerably. A few months can be just as rewarding if planned carefully while, if you have the time and funds, an extended trip can allow you to really explore the world. Be sure to give yourself enough time in each place and always add a few more days on than you think you actually need.

You may decide that you want to concentrate on one region of the world or try to fit in as many countries as possible. Whatever your philosophy, you need to try and balance your trip. Decide on the major sights or cities that you want to visit and then give yourself plenty of time around these to travel, relax or take in your surroundings. Try to plan a mixture of seeing attractions, adventure and just hanging out.

'You need to think carefully about where you want to go, how much you can realistically fit in and plan an itinerary.'

How do you get around the world?

Round-the-world flights

The most popular way to get across the world is by buying a round-the-world flight. These work out much cheaper than buying individual flights and are usually fairly flexible. There are various restrictions but the basic rules are similar to the following:

- You must start and end your journey in one place.
- You must keep travelling in the same direction around the world.
- Your ticket is valid for one year.
- You have to choose your destinations before you travel.

The best thing to do is talk to a travel agent as there are many different options and prices depending on how many stops you make, or which 'zones' you travel in. Your ticket is going to be cheaper if you stick to the major hubs and most popular destinations, for example:

- London – Bangkok – Sydney – LA – London.

Many passes also allow you to insert an overland segment so you can fly into one city and out of another within the same region. For example:

- London – Bangkok – overland to Singapore – Sydney – LA – overland to New York – London.

If you are going to do it this way you need to leave yourself plenty of time to travel between the two locations, or make sure that your ticket is flexible enough to allow date changes.

By sea

While a round-the-world flight is the cheapest and easiest option, circumnavigating the world by sea can be an awesome experience. Your choices are to travel by cruise ship (expensive), freighter ship (not very glamorous) or crewing a yacht (hard work). If you are serious about this idea then research your options and remember that it is only a good idea for those of you who have time on your hands and don't get seasick!

Overland

The most adventurous option is to travel overland. While this is easy in some parts of the world, others will prove more difficult and you either need to be a seasoned traveller or go with an organised tour. The best option is to throw in a few flights and combine them with some overland travel along the way.

Who will you travel with?

Travelling alone

Seeing you go off to travel the world alone is a parent's worst nightmare, but try to calm their nerves by reminding them that thousands of people go off travelling alone every year. As long as you are prepared and sensible, it can be a liberating experience and allow you to make all your own choices without having to compromise. There is a huge network of backpackers around the world who meet through hostels and continue their journeys together, so you won't be alone for long.

'The most rewarding part of my gap year was living with my host family and being accepted into another culture.'
Craig, 20.

Boy/girlfriends

Many people choose to take a gap year with their boyfriend or girlfriend. On one hand it is good to have the support of someone you are close to, but it is a very intense environment for a relationship to withstand. Nothing is going to ruin a gap year quicker than breaking up. If you have been together for a while then it may be a good way to test your staying power, while fledging couples are ill advised to set off together.

Friends

Travelling with a friend is quite similar to travelling with a boyfriend or girlfriend. You may get on really well when you see each other at school or hanging out at the weekends, but all day every day is a different matter. Think about it carefully and try to pick a trustworthy friend who you have known for a good amount of time. If you are planning to go with two or more friends then consider the group dynamics and the practicalities of making joint decisions.

Organised trips

'It's bad enough trying to decide what to pack for a week's holiday, let alone a year travelling the world. When you are going backpacking it is a whole new set of rules.'

The safest and most secure way to travel is to go on an organised tour. These will always cost more and allow less freedom, but will give you more support and guidance. Do your research to find out people's past experiences of the company and pick one that suits your age, interest and budget. Organised trips give you a ready made set of travel companions, so they can be a great idea if you are travelling alone.

What should you pack?

It's bad enough trying to decide what to pack for a week's holiday, let alone a year travelling the world. When you are going backpacking it is a whole new set of rules. You need items that multi-task and take up minimal space.

Backpack

Investing in good basic items will pay off. Choose a backpack that isn't too big for your frame and has good support and ventilation. Think about access to pockets and whether you can reach items without having to take the whole thing apart. Backpacks with detachable bags and straps are best. Karrimor and Eastpak are both trusted brands to consider but the most useful thing you can do is visit an outdoor supplies store such as Blacks (see help list) for some personal advice.

Clothing

Anyone trying to choose a year's worth of outfits is going to struggle, especially when you have to fit it all in one bag. Clothing needs to be multi-functional, take up minimal space and to not need ironing. Make sure you consider the climates and customs of the places you are visiting. Long sleeved cotton tops and trousers will always come in handy, as will any clothing that you can layer.

Other essentials

- Sleeping bag – choose a lightweight, compact one that is still warm and waterproof.

- Waterproof – it may not be the trendiest item but you will be thankful when you are waiting for your next bus in a downpour!

- Walking shoes – when you have been on your feet all day, having a good pair of walking shoes will seem like the best investment. These don't need to be expensive but should be supportive and waterproof.

- Torch – the dark can make anywhere seem scary, so make sure you have a good quality, compact torch to hand.

- Money belt – the safest place for your money is close to your body, so buy a belt that can fit snugly underneath your clothing.

- Water bottle and purifying tablets – investing in a sturdy water bottle will save you money and purifying tablets mean you will always have a supply of safe water to drink.

- A lock – as you will often be staying in shared accommodation and travelling by bus, a sturdy lock is an essential.

Use the packing checklist at the end of this chapter to make sure you have got everything you need. (For health and safety essentials, see chapter 4.)

Flights, visas and passports

You need to make sure that you have the basics in place so that you don't get caught out at the first hurdle.

Flights

Look for the best deals on flight comparison websites (see help list) and keep an eye on prices so you can book them when they drop. If you are making a number of different stops, it is usually much cheaper to buy a specialist round-the-world ticket. Check the restrictions as a lot of the round-the-world deals are quite flexible and allow you to change the dates and times along the way, while regular flights will not do this. Get into the habit of re-confirming your flight 48 hours beforehand.

Visas

Some countries require you to have a visa giving you permission to enter and stay there for a certain amount of time, especially if you are planning to work or study. Making sure that you have the right visa for each country that you will visit and for what you intend to do there is vital. Many countries, such as the United States, are very strict about these rules and if you are caught with the wrong visa you can be instantly sent home and banned from returning. Contact the embassy of the country you are planning to visit to find out what visa you may need, the process for getting one and how much it will cost. Costs will vary but they are generally a few hundred pounds. The best thing to do is apply for all your visas well in advance so you don't get caught out or have to think about it on the road. If your plans change while you are travelling then check that your visas are still valid. See www.projectvisa.com to get started.

Passports

Make sure that you have a valid passport that lasts for at least six months after the date you are going to return home. A new 10 year passport costs £77.50 and you can apply at your local post office or online at www.passport.gov.uk/passport. If it is your first passport, you will need to attend an interview. The whole process takes about six weeks. If you have had your passport for a while and the photo no longer resembles you closely, you should get it changed. To do this, you will have to renew your passport which costs the same as getting a new one but is worth the expense to save any confusion with immigration officials! It is essential to have two photocopies of your passport so you can leave one with your parents and take the other one away with you. You should always keep this copy in a separate place to the original.

Action points

- Do your research: find out what is on offer.
- Invest in good basic equipment.
- Visit www.roundtheworldflights.com to start planning your trip.
- Check that your passport is valid.
- Find out what visas you will need at www.projectvisa.com.

Packing checklist

Essential

- ☐ Walking shoes
- ☐ Waterproof
- ☐ Sleeping bag
- ☐ Torch
- ☐ Water bottle
- ☐ Towel
- ☐ Long sleeved top
- ☐ Lightweight trousers
- ☐ Short sleeved top
- ☐ Warm, thin jumper
- ☐ Swimwear
- ☐ Socks
- ☐ Underwear
- ☐ Sandals/flip flops
- ☐ Shorts
- ☐ Lock
- ☐ Photocopy of passport
- ☐ Toiletries
- ☐ Money belt

Recommended

- ☐ Lighter/matches
- ☐ Washing line
- ☐ Lightweight scarf
- ☐ Hat
- ☐ Sunglasses
- ☐ Ear plugs
- ☐ Sewing kit
- ☐ Power adaptors
- ☐ Pocket knife
- ☐ Phrasebooks and guidebooks
- ☐ Mosquito net
- ☐ Pillow
- ☐ Alarm clock
- ☐ Water purification tablets

Optional

- ☐ Camping mat
- ☐ Digital camera
- ☐ Plastic cutlery
- ☐ Photos from home
- ☐ Journal
- ☐ Address book
- ☐ Tent
- ☐ Mobile phone
- ☐ Mp3 player

Need2Know

Summing Up

To plan the best gap year, you need to get the basics right. Do your research to find out what is on offer and consider your options carefully, including who you will travel with, where you will go and how you will fund it. Invest in good basic equipment such as a backpack and sleeping bag and be realistic about what you can pack. Make sure that your passport is valid, that you have the right visas and that you have some idea of an itinerary. Once you have the practical issues in place, you can concentrate on planning a life changing gap year and enjoying what the world has to offer.

'Once you have the practical issues in place, you can concentrate on planning a life changing gap year and enjoying what the world has to offer.'

Chapter Two

Volunteering and Studying

Types of volunteer work

There are many different types of volunteer work, so it is worth considering which is right for you. This may be something that you are interested in, have experience of or just suits your skills or personality the best.

Working with children

Working with children is a popular choice for volunteer work and can be very rewarding. Whether it is teaching English, helping out in an orphanage or working with street children, the bonds you make will stay with you forever. However, try to remember that it can also be very heart wrenching to see the condition that some children live in – you need to learn not to get too attached.

Conservation

If you love animals or are keen on environmental issues then a conservation placement might be right for you. These usually take place in some of the world's most stunning places and give you access to areas you would never normally visit.

Specialist

Whether you are studying medicine, journalism or marine biology, there are opportunities to put your specialist skills to good use. Taking part in a specialist placement will be a boost to your CV and help you get a new perspective on your career choices.

Practical

Some people prefer to get their hands dirty and do some practical work. Whether it is digging wells or building houses, doing physical work leaves you with a tangible result to show for your efforts. It will be hard work and tiring but is a great way to feel like you have achieved something worthwhile.

'Whether it is digging wells or building houses, doing physical work leaves you with a tangible result to show for your efforts. It will be hard work and tiring but is a great way to feel like you have achieved something worthwhile.'

How do you choose a volunteer programme?

Search the Internet for volunteer placements and you will be bombarded with thousands of different options. So how do you know which one to go for? There are a number of things that you need to consider when deciding which programme to opt for.

Do your research so that you know what is available. Decide what is important to you and then ask questions so you can be clear about what you are signing up to. A good place to check for legitimate companies is www.theyearoutgroup.com where all the members have signed up to a code of practice. See the help list for some more reputable volunteer organisations.

Cost

Volunteer programmes can vary wildly in price. If you are booking one through a specialist company then you will be paying thousands of pounds, whereas if you arrange it locally it may only be a few hundred. The important thing is to know what you can afford, what your priorities are and what you are getting for your money.

Location

Due to the nature of volunteer work it is likely that you will be based in the poorest or most remote areas of the world, however location can still vary greatly. Think about whether you want to be in a city or rural location. This will affect the type of volunteer work that you are able to do. Do you have a particular country or area of the world that you are interested in? That is a good place to start.

Length of placement

Some people don't have the time or inclination to do a long term volunteer placement but would still like to have a go. There is a whole industry of volunteering for one or two weeks. Although many of these placements can work out to be expensive, they are convenient and allow you to get a taster without any commitment. However, to get the most out of any volunteer placement, you really need to do it for at least a month so that you can settle into your surroundings and get to know people. How long you commit to will depend on your own circumstances. You may decide to devote a whole year to volunteer work or choose a couple of different shorter placements.

Values and vision

If you have strong feelings or beliefs in certain areas then you ought to choose a volunteer placement that matches them. For example, if you are strongly religious you may want to choose a company that shares your values. Or perhaps you believe poverty should be dealt with in a certain way and want to work with an organisation that upholds your beliefs.

The best thing to do is talk to other people who have volunteered with the same organisation. There are many Internet forums where you can find people who are willing to share their experiences with you.

Values of volunteering

Volunteering is a very different kind of experience than just visiting a country. It is a great way to immerse yourself in the culture that you are visiting by getting to know local people and seeing the reality of life at ground level. You will get a true understanding of the places you visit rather than just skimming the surface or seeing them from a tourist's perspective.

Donating money to charity is great but helping out personally is a much more rewarding experience. It can give you a whole new perspective on life and make you question your own values and ideals. Putting yourself in an unfamiliar situation and presenting yourself with new challenges can teach you a lot about your strengths and capabilities. Volunteering is a great way to test your limits, develop your confidence and figure out who you are as a person. Your experiences will stay with you when you return home and help to shape your opinions on the world.

As well as being a great personal experience, volunteering can also boost your career. It gives you international experience in working with people of different cultures which is important in today's global workforce. You may also use your time volunteering to develop new skills such as teamwork and project management.

What should you expect?

It may sound obvious, but the places you will volunteer in will not be the same as home. It is easy to think that you will be fine but you need to be realistic about what you are signing up for and what you are able to handle. You may be in a remote area, very close to extreme poverty and living without running water – could you cope?

Accommodation

Because the nature of volunteer work often takes you to remote and poor locations, the accommodation you stay in is likely to be less modern than you are used to. It can vary greatly but you need to ask where you will be staying and decide what you are willing to experience. Would you be happy living with strangers who don't speak English? Can you cope without running water?

Work

While you have signed up to volunteer, you don't want to be taken advantage of. Find out what you will be expected to do and how many hours a day you will be committing to. Part of your trip is about seeing the country and experiencing the local culture, so you need to make sure you will have time to do this. Also, be sure that you are offered enough training to prepare you for the work you will be doing, whether this is on the job or before you start.

Poverty

A lot of the places you will volunteer in are going to be very poor. If you have not experienced extreme poverty before it can be a big shock to the system. Seeing it close up in person is very different to seeing it on the television and it is something you need to prepare yourself for. Remember that, although your volunteering will make a useful contribution, you are not going to be able to solve these people's problems.

Where is your money going?

A lot of volunteer programmes can be expensive, so it is important that you know where your money is going. If you organise it locally then your money should be going directly to the project. If you organise it through a big company then don't be afraid to ask questions:

- What percentage of your fee goes directly to the project?
- Where does the rest of it go?

'As well as being a great personal experience, volunteering can also boost your career. It gives you international experience in working with people of different cultures which is important in today's global workforce.'

- How is the money managed?
- What do you get for your fee?

Organising independently

Organising your volunteer work independently is not for the faint hearted but can be one of the best ways of doing it. It can save you a lot of money and ensure that what you are paying is going directly to those who need it.

'Cultural courses can be a brilliant way to find out more about the country that you are visiting. Whether it is a cooking course, dance or a local tradition, it can give you a great insight into the area.'

This option is not a good idea if you are an inexperienced traveller or have worried parents at home. Even if you have travelled a lot, you need to have your wits about you, trust your instinct and make sure you do a lot of research before you commit to anything.

While many big companies will make donations from your fee to the project, you may find that spending the same amount locally will do a lot more good.

Remember though, by organising volunteer work independently you don't have the back up or in-country support of a big organisation – you have to be comfortable looking after yourself and making your own decisions if things go wrong.

Studying

Another common thing to choose to do is study abroad. This may be to get stuck into the culture, pick up a new skill or learn a language and is a great way to meet other people and spend some quality time in one place. Embrace your chosen subject and make the most of any social events or extra activities that are run in conjunction with it. A popular way to study abroad is through a university programme, but there are also many private organisations that offer a great variety of courses abroad. For a comprehensive directory to start looking for ideas, try www.studyabroadlinks.com.

Language courses

Language courses are especially popular as being surrounded by a language is the best way to pick it up. It's also great to be able to communicate with the locals. These courses vary from a few days to months and can often be combined with a stint of volunteering. Try and give yourself a head start by learning a bit before you go, but be realistic about your level as being stuck in 'advanced Spanish' when you only know how to order a beer is not going to help you!

Cultural courses

Cultural courses can be a brilliant way to find out more about the country that you are visiting. Whether it is a cooking course, dance or a local tradition, it can give you a great insight into the area. These courses will usually be a bit shorter but, again, are often offered in conjunction with language courses or volunteering.

Skills

You may want to top up your skills to earn money while you are travelling or pursue or expand a hobby. Perhaps lifeguarding or outside survival is your kind of thing. Be sure you know exactly what the course will cover, check out their safety record and make sure that their certification is valid in other parts of the world.

Action points

- Think about what type of volunteer work would suit you.
- Ask key questions about the volunteer programme.
- Talk to other volunteers and check out recommendations.
- Find courses in the countries you want to visit.
- Check the safety record and accreditation of practical courses.

Questions to ask volunteer programmes

Experience

- [ ] What will I gain from it?
- [ ] What skills will I learn?
- [ ] What is the aim of the project?
- [ ] Who will I be helping?
- [ ] Can I talk to some past volunteers?

Conditions

- [ ] Where will I be staying?
- [ ] How easy is it to get around?
- [ ] Will I be sharing with others?
- [ ] What is the standard of accommodation?
- [ ] Are there any safety concerns?

Money

- [ ] How much will it cost?
- [ ] What does that include?
- [ ] How much more will I need?
- [ ] How much goes to the project?
- [ ] Where does the rest go?

Work

- [ ] What exactly will I be doing?
- [ ] How many hours will I work?
- [ ] What training will I receive?
- [ ] Who will I be working with?
- [ ] Is there in-country support?

Summing Up

Volunteering has become a very popular way to see the world and give something back. It allows you to immerse yourself in a culture, get to know the locals and see the reality of a country. Think about what kind of volunteer work would suit you and research suitable placements. Make sure that you are realistic about what to expect, the work involved and the commitment that you are making. If you are considering organising a placement independently, be sure you check the organisation out thoroughly and if going with a large company, find out where your money is going.

Chapter Three

Working

Unless you have another source of income, the chances are that you will have to work at some point during your gap year. You may choose to do this before you go away or combine it with your travels. Either way, there are a number of different options to consider and some exciting opportunities to gain more than just pocket money from your gap year job.

Seasonal work

Seasonal work is a popular way to earn some money and have some fun for a few months. Some people even make it a way of life; working a summer season somewhere sunny and then a winter season. Seasonal work doesn't usually pay very well but it is a great experience and your earnings will cover your expenses so you will not end up out of pocket. Across the world there are plenty of opportunities to take on seasonal agricultural work following the harvests. This kind of work, usually spending hours picking fruit or vegetables in the fields, is hard and not well paid. However, it is usually easy to pick up, very flexible and doesn't involve much thought or experience.

Summer season and holiday reps

Once the school holidays get started, thousands of families rush to holiday camps and resorts around the world. Summer camps in America are big business and you will be looking after a group of children while they enjoy an activity filled break. It is a good way to live and work in the country for a short amount of time and your visa will usually allow you an extra couple of weeks to travel around before flying home.

'Opportunity is missed by most people because it is dressed in overalls and looks like work.'
Thomas A. Edison.

Similar to camp supervisors, there are plenty of jobs as holiday reps. Not all are 18-30s style but can still be hard work and stressful. You will have to work all hours, dealing with guests' problems and complaints. However, you will get the chance to relax and have a bit of fun at the same time.

There are also many entertainment jobs available on holiday parks across the world. Whether you can sing, dance or juggle, it can be a fun way to spend your summer and a good learning ground if you want to develop your skills.

Winter season

Winter season work is usually based in and around ski resorts which are plentiful across Europe in countries including France, Switzerland and Austria. Further afield, Canada and the USA have some very big and well known resorts in places like Colorado and Banff (see help list for web resources). These resorts come alive as people flock to them over the winter months and they need a lot of staff to run them. Whether you have a specialist skill such as ski instruction or want to work in the bar or chalets, the bonus is that you are likely to be given a free ski pass so you can spend your free time on the slopes.

Teaching English

A popular way to earn some money is to teach English abroad. There are a lot of programmes that you can sign up to which take you to some amazing places. Usually you will have to be willing to commit to at least a few months but a year or more is more common.

Learning English is very popular across the world, so there are a lot of opportunities to work with both adults and children. Consider which age group you feel happiest teaching and also whether you want to be based in a school, community group or giving private lessons.

To teach English abroad you will usually need to have a TEFL qualification (see ESL Café in help list). You can pay to do this on your own or it will be included in the more prestigious programmes. During this training you will learn some techniques for teaching but you will also develop your own methods on the job. Before accepting a teaching position, check what you will be required to do, what class sizes and support you will have and how many hours you will have to work. Teaching English can be a very well paid occupation but remember that you will have to commit to it and it may limit the travelling that you are able to do.

Finding temporary work abroad

Many people decide to spend a period of time in one country and find some work while they are there to fund the rest of their travels. First, you need to check what restrictions there are on your visa as some will limit the amount of time you can work for one employer or the type of work you can do. Hospitality, administration and the travel industry are the most common areas to find work in, but you don't need to limit yourself to these. Start looking around for opportunities – ask other travellers, look for adverts in your hostel, scour the Internet and approach some employment agencies.

Working visas

Unfortunately, in most cases, working abroad is not as easy as just showing up and getting a job. With the EU regulation, working in Europe is fairly simple, but if you want to go further afield, you will need to apply for a work visa and requirements vary greatly.

Europe

Thanks to the European Union, it is easy to gain work across Europe without a visa. Anyone from a member of an EU country can go to another one and work without restrictions. If you are looking for temporary work as you travel, it is very useful to speak the language, although you can organise work through many UK companies without needing to know the language.

'Travelling the world and getting paid for it – what could be better than that?'

Melanie, talking about her time working on cruise ships.

Australia

Australia has long been the most popular destination for people on their gap years. As well as the sea and sunshine, its appeal has a lot to do with the ease of getting a working visa. If you are a British national under 30 you can apply for a working holiday visa. This means you can stay in Australia for up to 12 months and work for up to six months with each employer. You can apply online and have to enter Australia within 12 months of the visa being issued.

North America

America has notoriously strict immigration laws. If you are found working without an appropriate visa, you will be shipped back to England and banned from returning. Usually, both in America and Canada, the only way to do it is to apply through a recognised programme that will allow you to do seasonal work or organise work with a specific employer. There is not the option, as with Australia, of going over and picking up work while you are there.

Working in the UK

Internships

You may decide that instead of spending your gap year travelling, you would prefer to get a head start on your career. This will put you a step ahead of your peers and can be a great way to build invaluable contacts.

Firstly, you need to decide if you want to do an internship here or abroad. Internships are very popular in America and there are lots of opportunities over there.

You need to do your research and find out what programmes are available. If there is a particular company that you want to work for then find out how they recruit interns and put together a strong application.

Finding vacancies

Where do you start? If you are looking for a local job to save some money, look in the newspaper, visit the job centre or ask friends. You may want to consider joining some employment agencies as well who will look for suitable work for you.

If you want to work as an intern or trainee in a bigger firm then you will need to find out about schemes. Contact companies in the industry you are interested in and ask about vacancies. Most information will usually be on their websites, so that is a good place to start.

Writing a CV

Your CV is probably the first contact you will have with future employers, so it is important that it makes a great first impression. A CV needs to include details on your education and qualifications, work experience and any relevant pastimes. Don't panic if you have never had a job before, it is all about presenting your transferable skills.

Were you on the school council? That shows you can take on responsibility, make a commitment and work as part of a team. Are you a keen runner? That shows motivation and determination. Look at what you've done while you were at school and how those skills could help you in the world of work.

See the page overleaf for help on putting your own CV together.

How to write a CV

The basics

- Keep it short – ideally one page, no more than two.
- Use a simple layout and font.
- Use a sensible email address.
- Include entries with most recent first.
- Never lie.

Personal profile

Talk about your main attributes and skills, what work you are looking for and why you would be good at it.

Employment history

- Include company name, location, job title and date period you worked.
- Concentrate on what you learnt/were responsible for/added to the company – rather than the ins and outs of what you did daily.

Education

- Keep it concise – employers don't need to know about every module.
- Leave out the negative but never lie.

Achievements and skills

- Don't go too far back – a book prize you won in year 5 doesn't count!
- Stick to three or four points and don't exaggerate.
- Only include foreign languages if you can hold a basic conversation.

Hobbies

- Choose things that say something about your personality and capabilities – avoid hobbies like 'hanging out with friends'. Also, only include things you still do.

Need2Know

Working to save

In an ideal world, money would be no object. However, in reality you will need to think about how you are going to pay for your gap year. A popular route is to spend some of your year working at home to save up the money for travelling.

Getting into the habit of saving is the hardest part. You need to be strict with yourself and make a regular contribution to your savings account. Work out how much money you need to live on and then transfer the rest to a savings account as soon as you get paid. This will stop you having the temptation to spend it.

Your bank will be able to advise you on the best options and help you set up a savings account. Another good source of information and practical tips on saving money is www.moneysavingexpert.com.

Living at home

If you have just finished school and are planning your gap year, you are probably itching to get away from home. If you have been living away from home at university, then living with your parents again may not seem very appealing. However, when you are trying to save hard for your gap year, it is the best option.

Sit down with your parents and agree a set of rules that you are both happy with. They may want you to contribute towards the household costs, but it will still be a lot less than if you were living elsewhere. Try and be tolerant with each other and remember that it is only for a set amount of time.

Work and travel

Another option for working and travelling is to do both at the same time and choose a job that allows you to see the world. This is a bigger commitment than applying for a summer job or taking on some temporary work, but it also comes with some great opportunities.

'In an ideal world, money would be no object. However, in reality you will need to think about how you are going to pay for your gap year.'

Nanny

If you have a childcare qualification, it could be a great idea for you to become a nanny. Lots of families employ nannies to look after their children in the UK, abroad and while they travel. There are agencies that can help you find vacancies and organise visas and legalities for you such as Childcare International (see help list for details).

Cruise ships

Cruise ships offer a superb way of combining work and travel. There are all sorts of jobs – from waiters and bar staff to beauty therapists, photographers and sports coaches. Your food and accommodation will be taken care of so you don't have any expenses and can spend your money enjoying the amazing places you sail into.

You can apply for cruise ship jobs directly with the cruise line or through a hiring agent as they are always looking for new staff as the industry expands. Crown Recruitment is a good agency who hire for Royal Caribbean, Carnival and Azamara (see help list for details).

Crewing yachts

Having sailing experience is a bonus but yachts also need other staff such as chefs and cleaners. Crewing a yacht is hard work but can allow you to get a taste of the high life by visiting some of the world's wealthiest ports.

Most people find jobs in this line of work by turning up at ports and asking around but you can also look at www.crewseekers.net where many vacancies are advertised.

Action points

- Decide if you want to work at home or abroad.
- Work out what your skills and attributes are and spend time creating a CV.
- Do your research to find out what jobs are available.
- Make sure you have the appropriate working visa.

Summing Up

Most people will work at some point in their gap year to help them fund their time away. Whether you choose to work before you leave or take a job that allows you to travel or work abroad, you need to think carefully about your choice. You may decide to spend the whole time concentrating on working, in which case you need to do even more research to make sure you find a suitable job. There are some amazing opportunities to earn money while seeing the world and furthering your career, and a job doesn't just need to be a means to an end.

Chapter Four

Health and Safety

You want to remember your gap year for the rest of your life – but for all the right reasons. Catching a nasty disease, being mugged or left stranded abroad are probably not the type of memories you are planning to make. It may be the boring side of planning your trip, but making sure you are safe and healthy is essential if you want to enjoy all the fun parts. Check out what vaccinations you need for the areas of the world you are visiting and be aware of common scams and mishaps so that you can do your best to prevent them from happening to you.

Disease prevention

It is important that you take the correct precautions against disease and get the right vaccinations for wherever in the world you are travelling. Sometimes you can get these for free from your GP, otherwise you may have to pay.

For some areas of the world, certain precautions are essential while others may only be advised, especially if you are just visiting certain parts of a country. Make sure you visit your GP at least eight weeks before you are due to travel so you have time to get everything you need.

Malaria

Malaria is a serious disease that you catch from mosquito bites in many tropical areas. Wearing long clothing, using a strong mosquito spray and a mosquito net can all help prevent you catching it, but you should also take a course of malaria tablets. You will need to start these before you go to the affected area and continue taking them once you leave.

'It is important that you take the correct precautions against disease and get the right vaccinations for wherever in the world you are travelling.'

Yellow fever

Yellow fever is a viral infection transmitted by mosquitoes and is most common in Sub-Saharan Africa and tropical areas of South America. The vaccine is one simple injection that lasts around 10 years and some countries require proof that you have been vaccinated before they will let you in.

Hepatitis A

Hepatitis A is caught from contaminated food and water or from person to person through poor hygiene. Make sure that the water you drink is safe and avoid anything that may have been washed in contaminated water such as salad or fruit. A vaccination will protect you for up to a year and then a booster shot will make sure you are covered for the next 20 years.

Typhoid

Typhoid is caused by salmonella bacteria through food that has been contaminated with faeces or urine. A single vaccine will protect you for up to three years.

Meningococcal meningitis

Meningococcal meningitis is passed on through respiratory excretion such as coughing or sneezing. It is difficult to prevent but you can get a vaccine against it which is advised if you are visiting areas where there have been outbreaks e.g. Saudi Arabia, India, Nepal and some parts of Sub-Saharan Africa.

Tetanus and polio

Both of these diseases are vaccinated against under the child immunisation programme, so most people should already be protected. If you have not had these vaccinations or are at particular risk, talk to your GP.

Jetlag

When you are travelling around the world you are going to enter lots of time zones and gain and lose hours as you go. All these time changes can take their toll on your body. There are various schools of thought about how to deal with jetlag but having a sleep on the plane, avoiding alcohol and drinking lots of water will all help. Trying to regulate your body clock by staying up until night time in your new location will also help you get over it a bit quicker.

Altitude sickness

Some popular tourist destinations – e.g. Cusco and Machu Picchu in Peru – are at a much higher altitude than you are probably used to. While some people won't notice any difference, others can be affected quite severely by altitude sickness which can leave you feeling dizzy, sick and disorientated. The best way to combat it is to acclimatise slowly at intermediate altitudes and go back down if you are feeling unwell. There are altitude sickness tablets you can take – Acetazolamide being a common one – or in South America, chewing coca leaves is the accepted remedy.

Safe sex

Safe sex is essential wherever you are in the world and the best way to stay safe is to plan ahead.

- Condoms – the best thing to do is to take a supply of condoms with you from the UK. If you are going to buy them abroad, make sure that they have the CE symbol that means they meet European standards, or choose well known, respected brands if further afield. If you decide to sleep with someone then make sure that a condom is used.

- The pill – if you are on the pill, visit your GP and get a supply for your whole trip. When you are travelling with a lot of time changes, knowing when to take your pill can be confusing. Try to do the maths and take your pill within 12 hours of the normal time. Remember that the pill does not protect you against sexually transmitted infections (STIs).

'There are various schools of thought about how to deal with jetlag but having a sleep on the plane, avoiding alcohol and drinking lots of water will all help.'

- STIs and AIDS – nobody can be counted as 'safe' because of what they look like or where they come from so you always need to protect yourself. If you think that you may have contracted an STI, you need to find a local clinic and get checked out as it may get worse if you leave it until you return home.

What precautions should you take?

Trying to fit all your clothes in your backpack may seem hard enough, but you need to make sure that you leave room for a few safety essentials. Having the basics to hand can make a big difference when you are in a tricky situation and prevention is always better than cure.

Mosquito spray

If you are visiting humid countries, the jungle or anywhere known for mosquitoes, you need to buy some good repellent. Not only will bites leave you in a lot of discomfort, you also run the risk of catching malaria – not a fun prospect. Be sure to spend the extra pounds on a strong spray that contains a high percentage of DEET (the most common active ingredient found in insect repellent) as many others have little effect.

Safety alarm

Although no substitute for staying safe, a safety alarm can be a good back-up and help you gain attention if you find that your safety is threatened. There are many options but a pocket sized alarm with a strap to attach to your bag can be the most practical choice. Some police stations or student unions give these out for free, so it is worth checking before you buy one.

Emergency numbers

Do you know how to phone for an ambulance in Thailand? It is a good idea to check what the local emergency numbers are in the countries that you are visiting. Also, make sure you know how to contact your local embassy and have the number of your travel insurance company handy.

First aid pack

Having some basics with you will be helpful when you get a blister, cut or graze and don't have access to any medical supplies. A basic first aid pack should include:

- Plasters.
- Bandages.
- Antiseptic cream.
- Cotton wool.
- Sterile dressings.
- Adhesive tape.
- Disposable gloves.
- Scissors.
- Tweezers.
- Safety pins.

It is also a good idea to go on a first aid course so that you know how to deal with emergency situations and carry out basic procedures.

See the end of the chapter for a complete health and safety checklist which will ensure that you are fully prepared.

Diarrhoea and rehydration tablets

You may have heard of 'Delhi belly' and it sounds quite funny until you actually experience it! Because the quality of the water is not as good in some countries and you will be eating different foods, you can be prone to getting diarrhoea. As well as being very uncomfortable, it can quickly lead to dehydration, so it is good to have the ability to minimise its effect.

Painkillers and allergy pills

Yes, you will be able to buy painkillers abroad but it is much easier to deal with brands and doses that you are familiar with. It is also a good idea to take some allergy pills as you never know what you may have an adverse reaction to.

Safe travel

'Natural disasters can be difficult to predict but it is worth checking for any details on recent activity in places you are planning to visit.'

Across the world there is a lot of political instability and you should always check with the foreign office for advice on which countries are safe to travel to. While some are quite obvious, there can be unrest in regions that you are unaware of and certain areas of countries should be best avoided, even if the rest of it is safe to travel to.

Terrorism

Unfortunately, terrorism is a realistic concern in today's world. Part of the terror is that you cannot predict the attacks and there really is nowhere that you can consider 'safe'. This is not meant to scare you but to point out that you should not let your fears stop you from travelling as an attack could just as well happen in your home town. Security has increased in airports and major tourist destinations but it is still worth being vigilant and reporting any suspicious activity.

Natural disasters

There have been some major natural disasters in recent years and nobody could have failed to be shocked by the Tsunami that devastated areas of Asia. Like terrorism, natural disasters can be difficult to predict but it is worth checking for any details on recent activity in places you are planning to visit. Take note of any serious weather warnings, make sure you are adequately prepared and do not take unnecessary risks by thinking it won't happen to you.

Drug smuggling

You have no doubt seen the stories on the news of young people being sentenced to life in jail for drug smuggling abroad. Some people choose to take that risk while others are coerced into it – but the authorities often do not care about your reasons. Many foreign jails have terrible conditions and it is not somewhere you want to end up. Even a recreational amount of cannabis can land you in serious trouble, so be very careful about using drugs abroad – the best way to stay safe is by not being involved with drugs at all!

Scams

It would be nice to think that everybody is friendly and helpful, and most are, but unfortunately there is still a small percentage who are out to rip you off. It is good to meet new people and socialise with the locals, but you also need to be aware of some common scams.

- Fraud – whether it is your passport or your bank card, you need to be extra careful when you are abroad. A common scam is for a shopkeeper to take your card into the back in order to scan it and then get you to sign the receipt. While they are back there though, they make an extra copy for a further amount and then forge your signature. Always ask them to bring the machine out to where you can see it.

- Keep your luggage with you – when you are travelling around the world your luggage is the home of all your worldly possessions and the last thing you want to do is lose them. Some dodgy taxi drivers will wait for you to get out and then drive off with your luggage in their boot. Instead, keep it with you on the seat of the car.

- Check your change – when you are dealing with a foreign currency it is easy to get confused and not be exactly sure how much things cost or how much change you are due. Some retailers will take advantage of this by short changing you, so try to be aware of what you are owed and count it before you leave.

- Stick with your hotel – a lot of travellers have found that when they give the address of their hotel or hostel to a taxi driver, they claim that it no longer exists. They may seem helpful, offering to take you to a different one, but this is a scam and they will be on commission to take tourists to it. Check in advance that the place exists by calling them or looking on the Internet, then be firm with your taxi driver that you want to be taken to it.

'When I had my bag stolen in South America I was so happy that my mum had badgered me into getting travel insurance.'

Ele, 18.

Travelling alone

Travelling alone can be a scary prospect – often more for your parents than for you! Plenty of people do it every year but you need to make sure that you stay safe and don't put yourself in any unnecessary danger. Tell someone where you are going to be and inform your hostel or another traveller if you are going anywhere remote.

It is a good idea to make sure that you always have a charged mobile phone with you and stay in regular touch with friends and family at home so they know where you are. Also, be sure you have enough cash to make a call or catch a taxi in an emergency.

Be careful not to give too much personal information away to strangers and be wary about telling taxi drivers that you are travelling alone. Stay in reputable hostels and make sensible travel choices so you don't end up in any sticky situations.

Need2Know

Women travellers

In certain areas of the world, women may need to adapt their behaviour and dress appropriately in order to respect local customs. In more conservative countries, women are expected to cover up completely. It is advisable to act in a moderate way to avoid any unwanted attention.

Wherever you are travelling, it is important as a female traveller, to be sensible – don't walk alone at night, only use reputable travel firms and be careful about who you befriend. If you make responsible choices there is no reason why you cannot have a safe, fun experience travelling alone.

Trusting your instinct

If something doesn't feel right then it probably isn't. Trusting your instinct is one of the best things that you can do to stay safe. Our 'sixth sense' acts as an early warning system as our unconscious mind registers danger before our conscious mind has a chance to notice. Don't feel stupid or scared for trusting your instinct. You want your gap year to be a fun and memorable experience for all the right reasons and erring on the side of caution will help keep it that way.

Action points

- Check the foreign office website for up-to-date travel advisories.
- Visit your GP at least eight weeks before you set off to get all the relevant vaccinations.
- Make a simple health and safety kit.
- Never put yourself in an unnecessarily dangerous situation.
- Trust your instinct.

Health and safety checklist

Essential

- [ ] Vaccinations
- [ ] Vaccination certificates
- [ ] Mosquito repellent
- [ ] Antiseptic wipes
- [ ] Plasters
- [ ] Painkillers
- [ ] Allergy pills
- [ ] Diarrhoea tablets
- [ ] Sunscreen
- [ ] Travel insurance policy
- [ ] Emergency contact numbers
- [ ] Prescription medication

Recommended

- [ ] Condoms
- [ ] Safety alarm
- [ ] Malaria tablets
- [ ] Cold medicine
- [ ] Indigestion remedies
- [ ] Rehydration sachets
- [ ] Insect bite cream
- [ ] Tweezers
- [ ] Blister plasters

Optional

- [ ] Contraceptive pill
- [ ] Sanitary products
- [ ] Toilet paper
- [ ] Bandages
- [ ] Cystitis relief
- [ ] Altitude sickness medicine

Need2Know

Summing Up

Health and safety may be the boring bit but is also the most important in making sure your trip runs smoothly. The last thing you want to do is abandon your gap year because of something that you could have prevented. Make sure that you find out about the places you want to visit, how safe they are and what vaccinations you will need. As well as carrying essential health and safety items with you, trust your instinct and don't put yourself in any situations that may be unsafe.

'Health and safety may be the boring bit but is also the most important in making sure your trip runs smoothly. The last thing you want to do is abandon your gap year because of something that you could have prevented.'

Chapter Five

Money

Planning for a gap year is an exciting time but paying for it can be a little less enjoyable! Whatever you decide to do with your year, you need to think about how you are going to pay for it.

How much money will you need?

How much you spend can vary wildly depending on the level of luxury that you are looking for and whereabouts in the world you are going. Costs for different areas of the world are covered in their relevant chapters further along in the book, but an average daily budget, staying in hostels, eating reasonably and having a few trips and activities would be around £15-20 for developing countries and £35-40 for developed countries.

To work out how much money you are going to need for your trip you need to do your research. Find out average prices for flights, accommodation, volunteer programmes and any other major costs in the areas of the world you want to visit. Then look at the cost of living for each place and how much you will need for everyday expenses while you are there. On top of that you need to add some money for activities, socialising, treats and emergency funds.

Flights

Flights are going to be your biggest single cost, so it is important that you get the best deal. Some round-the-world flights offer great savings and can be found for as little as £800. Check out www.roundtheworldflights.com to find the best value flight for your trip or talk to a travel specialist such as Trailfinders (see help list for details). If you go on the most common routes, e.g. Asia – Australia – America, then it can be quite cheap, but once you start adding less popular places, it can soon add up. As you will book your major flights before you leave, you will already have paid this expense. However, you still need to leave some money for any flights you may want to take locally.

Other travel

Once you have arrived in a country, you are still going to need to travel around it. Travelling by bus is usually the cheapest option but if you are going to travel long distances in Australia or America, it can be worth buying a car or camper van and selling it when you are done.

Equipment

It is worth investing in a good backpack as it can make a big difference to your comfort. The same goes for a sleeping bag and a good pair of walking shoes. These costs will need to be paid out before you leave but will definitely give you your money's worth (see chapter 1 for information on buying equipment).

Accommodation

The cost of your accommodation can vary wildly. Camping is the cheapest but in some areas it is not safe to do so. There are hostels available in all backpacker destinations but the quality can be very different, so it is good to find recommendations. If you would like to treat yourself to some better accommodation along the way, make sure you have budgeted it in.

- Camping – as the cheapest way to bed down for the night you may choose to stay on a campsite, or set up in an unofficial location. The downside of camping is that you will have to carry your equipment with you and this can add a lot of extra bulk and weight to your backpack.

- Home stays – home stays are popular if you are volunteering or learning a language and can be a cost-effective way to stay and get to know the locals. Families will usually be assigned by the organisation you book with.

- Couch surfing – there has been a growth in 'couch surfer' websites, where other travellers agree to let you stay in their homes. Many of the popular

'Travelling by bus is usually the cheapest option but if you are going to travel long distances in Australia or America, it can be worth buying a car or camper van and selling it when you are done.'

sites such as www.couchsurfing.org have review sections where you can see what other people have said about the hosts. This is by no means a guarantee of safety but can help you vet people.

- Hostels – hostels are the most popular kind of accommodation for travellers. They are plentiful and can be found in every city or tourist trail in the world. The cost and standard can vary wildly, so it is good to get recommendations or stick to listings in trusted guide books. You will usually be sleeping in a same sex dorm but in some hostels it is possible to book a private room at an extra cost, which can work out well if you are travelling with a partner or friends.

- Guesthouses – guesthouses are often small, family-run places that have been set up in a home. They usually offer good value for money and include breakfast. If you are travelling alone this can work out expensive but with friends or a partner, it can be a reasonable option.

- Hotels – although you may associate hotels with expense, you can get a lot more for your money in some areas of the world. You may also find that after months in shared hostels, you might be willing to splash out a little bit more for a night of comfort.

Programmes and visas

If you are going on an organised volunteering or work programme, this is going to be a big expense which you will have to pay for in advance. Make sure that you do your research and know what is included in the cost as the extra expenses can all add up. Consider the cost of living for the region you will be staying in so you can work out how much more money you may need.

If you need to get a visa to work in or visit a country, you need to consider that expense too. Find out how much these will cost in advance so you are fully prepared and can factor it into your budget.

Trips

While travelling, you may decide to take a trip because you don't have much time, are travelling alone or want to go somewhere difficult to reach. The price of trips will depend on where you are in the world and whether you book it locally. Look into costs in advance and make sure you know what you are getting for your money and if you will have to pay out anything extra for food or activities. While you can always find someone who will do it for less, remember that the cheapest isn't always the best value.

Food

You have to eat, so this area of budgeting is essential! If you are happy to make your own meals and buy food from markets, you can get by on quite a small budget. However, if you would like the occasional meal out, or are travelling in more expensive countries such as America or Europe, then it can become a major expense.

'A few basic meals and some lacklustre hostels meant I could afford the really memorable moments.'

Sarah, 22

Activities

Travelling around the world gives you the opportunity to experience some amazing activities. Decide on the things that you really want to do and make sure that you have enough money to do them so that you are not left disappointed. Be careful about going for the cheapest providers as you want to make sure they are safe and reliable. The best thing to do is to ask other travellers or enquire at your hostel.

Part of the fun of travelling is meeting new people and you are going to want to socialise. A few drinks in a local bar is not going to break your budget, but you need to make sure that you don't build your budget too tightly to have a bit of fun. Hostels often have reasonably priced drinks and will arrange social events. In tourist areas, prices will shoot up, so you may only want to hang out there for one slowly sipped drink!

Travel insurance

Travel insurance is not an area to scrimp on. Of course you hope that nothing bad will happen but if it does, you want to make sure you can access the best help available. Your bank or home insurer may be able to offer you travel insurance but some companies will only insure travellers for shorter trips. Shop around for the best deals on a comparison site such as Insure My Trip (see help list for details).

Insurance will cost more if you are travelling outside Europe and many companies have a further premium for travelling in North America. By agreeing to pay a higher amount yourself before the company pays out, you will be able to lower the cost of your insurance. Never lie about any details on your application as this can invalidate your claim.

- Sports cover – remember that most policies will not cover any kind of sports or high risk activity unless you pay extra. This means that all the bungee jumping, sky diving and white water rafting that you want to do won't be covered unless you specifically buy insurance for it.

- Repatriation and medical bills – in some countries, such as the United States, medical bills can be astonishingly high, so you don't want to run the risk of having to pay them. Take a look at how much the insurance covers and if anything – such as pre-existing conditions – is excluded. Also, find out whether it only covers in-country treatment or if it will pay for repatriation back to the UK.

- Personal items – cheaper travel insurance policies will not give any cover for the loss of personal items and those that do will have set limits and often group items together under one claim. Read the fine details of these and if you are travelling with an expensive camera or other equipment, make sure it is named separately.

Managing your money

Once you have worked out how much money you are going to need for your gap year, you can start figuring out how you are going to save it. Perhaps you have savings, your parents are willing to contribute to your trip or you are planning to work while you are away to contribute to your fund. If you still need to save money before you leave then you must work out how much you can afford to put aside and regularly transfer this to a savings account.

How do you budget?

While you are away you need to keep an eye on what you are spending. If you only have limited funds, the last thing you want to do is run out of money half way round the world! By working out a weekly budget and sticking to it, you will make sure that you have enough spare cash to spend on the exciting stuff. Use the budgeting form at the end of this chapter to work out how much money you will have to work with, then keep a log of what you spend so you can see where your money is going. It is easy to get carried away when you are travelling – remember to concentrate on your priorities and make sure you have money for the things you really want to do.

Keeping money safe

Whether you are at home or thousands of miles away, you should always be keeping your money safe. However, when you have been away for a while it can be easy to get a bit blasé about where you stash your cash. The best thing you can do is buy a money belt which will sit flat under your clothes so your money is always close by. If you are staying in communal accommodation, make sure you have a locked compartment to keep it in.

Access to money

When you are travelling you want to make sure that you always have enough money. You also need to be careful about how much money you have on you at once. The best way to handle it is to have a combination of different methods. You should always make sure that you have a reasonable amount of cash on you so that you are not caught out. In most areas of the world though, you will be able to access your money at a cash point and this often gives you the best exchange rate. However, it is good to have a back-up in case you lose your card or it does not work. Take a few travellers cheques with you in sterling or US dollars so you can cash them anywhere.

Changing currency

As you travel around the world you are probably going to need a number of different currencies. It is not worthwhile leaving home with all of these – instead pick them up along the way. One of the easiest ways to get money in different countries is to use your cash card. Travelling with some US dollars is also a good idea as many people often prefer to receive these than their local currency.

When you do need to change money you can visit a bank or travel exchange, or many hotels or hostels will also run this service. Before changing any money, have an idea of what the current exchange rate is so that you do not get a bad deal. You will always have to pay some sort of charge, so plan how much you will need as you go along to avoid making too many small transactions and losing out.

Money saving tips

- Flights – keep checking sites as prices can change a lot. Have a look just after midnight when tickets are released and mid-week when prices are often lower.

- Accommodation – staying out of the centre is always cheaper. Keep your eyes open for special offers and consider taking up those offers of a sofa to sleep on from friends you have made along the way.

- Food – go where the locals go, avoid the tourist areas and look for 'meal of the day' offers. Buy food from the street vendors and local markets and make use of cooking facilities in hostels.

- Activities and attractions – look out for discount cards, student discounts and money off vouchers. Take advantage of any free museums and galleries or specific days or evenings when they offer discounted entry.

- Shopping – bargaining is common in many countries and is to be expected. Make sure you are not showing a lot of wealth through your dress or jewellery, then decide what you want to pay and start significantly lower to give haggling room.

'One of the easiest ways to get money in different countries is to use your cash card. Travelling with some US dollars is also a good idea as many people often prefer to receive these than their local currency.'

Action points

- Open a savings account and set up a monthly direct debit.

- Use the form opposite to work out how much money you will have.

- Buy a money belt and keep your money safe and secure at all times.

- Find out the cost of living for each destination (see continent guides).

- Create a weekly budget.

Need2Know

Budgeting

Overall budget

Money from savings

Money from parents

Amount you expect to earn before you go

Amount you expect to earn while travelling

Total

Expenses

Flights

Other travel

Equipment

Accommodation

Programmes and visas

Trips

Food

Socialising

Activities

Travel insurance

Emergency funds

Total

Travelling budget

Daily cost of living

Number of days

Total

Summing Up

Money makes the world go round and helps you go around the world. It would be great if you had an endless supply but the chances are you will need to budget and prioritise. Do your research so you know how much the cost of living will be in the areas of the world you are visiting. Then try and work out how much money you will need – leaving some room for activities, socialising and emergencies. Make sure that you keep your money safe and always have access to some back up funds.

Chapter Six

Asia

Popular with gap year travellers for its cheap hostels and backpacking trail, Asia is a continent that offers culture, relaxation and value for money. Step away from the tourist trail and you will find genuine, welcoming people who make this continent what it is. Fabulous food, ancient sites and beautiful beaches have marked Asia as a firm favourite.

Where to go

When you think of travelling in Asia you are probably automatically drawn to Thailand or India, but the continent stretches all the way over to Saudi Arabia and Yemen. The most popular area is still Southeast Asia where you can fly into the hub of Bangkok and spend your time on the beaches of Thailand. Circle north to take in the culture of Vietnam and Cambodia or pick the clean class of Singapore and head south to enjoy the beauty of Indonesia. If the language and traditions of the east intrigue you, fly into high-rise Hong Kong before stepping out into the sprawl of China and up to Beijing to walk on the Great Wall. Fly over to Japan to get a taste of its intriguing past and the high-tech future before flying on out of Tokyo. It is possible to spend your whole trip just in India which can prove to be addictive with its mix of people, food, landscapes and culture. If you are feeling more ambitious, head over to the Middle East but make sure you have done your research to navigate this less travelled region.

'India is the cradle of the human race, the birthplace of human speech, the mother of history, the grandmother of legend, and the great grand mother of tradition.'

Mark Twain.

What to see

Taj Mahal, India

This iconic mausoleum in Agra is just as impressive close up – if you can see it clearly through the hazy smog caused by pollution in the city.

Hong Kong at night

The lights on the high-rise buildings reflect in the river and present an image in sharp contrast with the small boats and homes that float on it.

Reclining Buddha, Thailand

There is more to Bangkok than cheap bars and hostels and this striking Buddha, the largest in Thailand, sits in Bangkok's oldest Buddhist temple.

Washing in the Ganges, India

The mass of Hindus making the pilgrimage to perform the traditional washing away of their sins in this sacred river is a dazzling sight to see.

Angkor Wat Temple, Cambodia

This collection of over one hundred temples dating from the 12th century is overrun by the jungle and looks like something out of an Indiana Jones movie.

Things to do

Have a curry on the beach

Curry may be the UK's national dish but what better place to eat it than where it originated, combined with the other love of the Brits – sun, sea and sand.

Get a suit tailor-made in Hong Kong

Look like you can afford a trip to Saville Row by investing in the super talented but cut price services of a tailor in Hong Kong or Thailand.

Ride on an elephant

It may not be the most comfortable of rides but riding on an elephant has to be the ultimate in exotic travel!

Walk along the Great Wall of China

Stretching around 4,000 miles, it's the only manmade structure that can be seen from space – that should be reason enough to take a bit of a stroll.

Buy some silks

Whether you want to use them as a scarf, for curtains or as a present for your mum, the silks in Asia are stunning.

'Fabulous food, ancient sites and beautiful beaches have marked Asia as a firm favourite.'

Customs, laws and language

Asia is the largest and most populated continent (it is home to 60% of the world's population) and with this comes a diverse mix of countries and cultures. From the conservative societies of the Middle East to cosmopolitan hubs like Hong Kong and Singapore and the world powerhouse of China, there is no one set of rules that will cover you for them all.

Southeast Asia is very popular with backpackers for its spiritual, laid back approach to life and the friendly welcoming nature of its people. Initially, India can be a bit overwhelming but if you strip away the outer images, you will find an enchanting set of people. In China and Japan you will find that people are much more proud and private and it may take you a little longer to get to know them.

'The main hubs of Asia are usually included on a round-the-world ticket, so it pays to stop off at places such as Bangkok, Hong Kong or Singapore.'

In Japan and Hong Kong and the major cosmopolitan cities, you can get away with speaking English but if you are travelling into mainland China or countries such as Cambodia, you will struggle without a few simple phrases. Obviously, Japanese and Chinese are not the easiest languages to learn but you should be able to pick up a few phrases even if you can't read it.

Areas further west and in the Middle East are much more conservative and strictly religious. A lot of countries in this area are Muslim and have conservative views about dress and behaviour. Make sure you have long, loose fitting clothes and women should have something to cover their head. If you are going to visit these areas, be careful not to behave by western standards. Alcohol is often forbidden and you can be locked up for being too intimate in public. The main language is Arabic but English is widely spoken.

Getting there and getting around

The main hubs of Asia are usually included on a round-the-world ticket, so it pays to stop off at places such as Bangkok, Hong Kong or Singapore. The area has also been receiving more low cost airlines, so even if you are travelling directly or within the region, you can find some good deals. Try www. airasia.com or www.jetstarasia.com.

Japan and China have extensive rail networks but outside of these countries you will probably be relying on the bus system, taking a few internal flights or choosing an organised tour. There are many companies that serve this region of the world but they vary in price considerably depending on whether they are run locally or by a foreign company.

Health and safety

There has been a lot of unrest in this region recently, so it's important to check for foreign office travel advisories before visiting any of the more unstable countries such as Sri Lanka or Tibet. However, Southeast Asia is generally a fairly safe destination for travellers.

In China there has been a lot of tension about human rights issues and although it is safe to travel around, you may be wise to bite your tongue sometimes so you don't cause offence or get in trouble with the authorities.

There are a number of vaccinations recommended for this area of the world, so check in with your GP who will be able to advise you on what you need. The basic recommendations are hepatitis A, hepatitis B, tetanus, measles and typhoid vaccinations. You also need to be careful about what you eat and drink in the region as no one wants to suffer the infamous Delhi belly! Try to stick to bottled water and avoid any food that may have been washed in water or seems poorly cooked.

Costs

Although it can cost quite a lot to get there, once you are in Asia, living is quite cheap (depending greatly on which country you are visiting). While your money will go a long way in Thailand and India, you won't get much for it in the likes of Dubai or the bigger cities in the region. You can live for as little as £5 a day in India, Nepal and Indonesia, but this can easily jump to over £30 if you are staying somewhere more cosmopolitan.

Accommodation and food costs vary wildly depending on what level of luxury you are looking for. This area of the world has some of the most expensive hotels in the world – in Dubai for example – and also some of the cheapest backpacking hostels. You can pick up some amazing street food or enjoy a curry on the beach in Goa for next to nothing, while some people will be splashing out hundreds of pounds for a meal in a top restaurant.

Asia is a great place for picking up silks and clothing. In Thailand and Hong Kong you can get a suit made for a fraction of the price you would pay for the service in the UK. It is a good idea to carry some US dollars with you as these are often popular, especially if you are buying produce at the markets.

Living and working

Asia is a common destination for people wanting to teach English and there are a number of relatively well paid programmes in Japan, www.jetprogramme. org being a popular one. You will also find a lot of volunteer programmes in the region, many working with children or animals. You should do your research before signing up to any of these but they are a great way to really get to see the local culture.

In recent years, Dubai and the Middle East have been attracting a lot of work, and people are drawn out there because of the tax free living. They are not the best places to pick up casual work but if you are planning to spend a solid portion of your time working, they can be a great place to work and save.

Action points

- Budget more for visits to the cosmopolitan cities in the region.
- Pack layers and long clothes for conservative countries.
- Check with the foreign office for any civil unrest.
- Learn a few key phrases for countries where you can't guess at the language.
- Pick areas that suit your personality.

Summing Up

There are some well worn backpacker roads in Asia and it is a laid back and spiritual place to travel. Don't find yourself limited to the south east though as there is plenty to see further afield. Start your trip from one of the cosmopolitan hubs such as Bangkok and Hong Kong but make sure you experience the countryside and culture away from the big cities. Head in the direction that suits your interests and personality – whether it is partying, culture or relaxation.

- Watch: *The Beach* directed by Danny Boyle.

- Read: *Wild Swans: Three Daughters of China* by Jung Chang.

- Surf: www.thingsasian.com.

Chapter Seven

Africa

Africa is often associated with poverty and corruption but once you have experienced its power, you will be addicted. Only a small step from Europe, it is a whole different world that will assault your senses and give you a new reality check. From the pyramids and souks in North Africa to the vast stretches of desert and vibrant city of Cape Town, Africa will enchant you.

Where to go

A popular and relatively safe place to start is Cape Town which has a great laid back trendy appeal. Move east along the famous garden route or north to Kruger National Park for some animal spotting. From here you can continue up to see the stunning Victoria Falls in Zambia, the dunes of Namibia or the 'warm heart of Africa' by heading up to Malawi. Most people go to Africa for safari where Kenya and Tanzania are the best bet. This area is also good for a quick beach break by popping over to the Kenyan resorts or on to Zanzibar. North Africa also offers some great sights – from the pyramids in Egypt, over to the souks of Marrakech in Morocco. If you're feeling adventurous, head south from here and take in the whole of the continent which is much more about the people and the experience than ticking things off along the way.

'The person who has not travelled widely thinks his or her mother is the only cook.'

African proverb.

What to see

Massai Mara, Kenya

This immense national reserve is especially famous for its views of the formidable wilderbeast migration.

Table Mountain, South Africa

Looming over Cape Town, the hanging mist makes this imposing mountain look all the more impressive.

The Pyramids, Egypt

A wonder of the ancient world, the pyramids are a truly unique site and cannot be seen anywhere else in the world.

Mount Kilimanjaro, Tanzania

Even if you don't have the time, inclination or money to climb it, a trip to Mount Kilimanjaro is still mesmerising.

Victoria Falls, Zambia

Straddling the border of Zambia and Zimbabwe, the immense amount of water tumbling over these falls is scary.

Things to do

Feel lost in the Namibian desert

With the largest sand dunes in the world, it is difficult to know which way is out! It is an awesome feeling to be just a dot in the desert.

Buy some local crafts

Some of the local indigenous crafts are so intricate and based on generations of experience that you will always have a unique souvenir.

Go on safari

There's nothing quite as amazing as watching a lion or giraffe in their natural habitat. It may be a bit pricey but it's worth every penny.

Ride a camel

It's not particularly comfortable but it is a unique experience that you won't get on the beach at Blackpool.

Start haggling in the souks

Unlike in your local supermarket, haggling is an expected part of the culture and can bag you a great bargain!

Customs, laws and language

Africa is often portrayed as a scary continent and although there has been a lot of war and corruption over the years, it is still a great place to visit.

The majority of people are humble and hardworking and are also very hospitable, despite often being very poor themselves. Generally, wherever you go, you will be made to feel welcome by the infectious charm of the locals. Many countries are still very conservative, especially in the Muslim areas of the north, so it is important to respect their cultures and cover up.

There are a wide range of languages and dialects spoken across Africa but French is prevalent in the west. In the majority of places, even in small remote villages, you will be able to get by with English and a few signs and actions!

'Out of all the places I visited, Africa was the one that got under my skin and I can't stop thinking about.'
James, 27.

Getting there and getting around

Flights to Africa can be expensive and although they can be included on round-the-world tickets, they are not the most common and therefore push the price up. It can be worth travelling to France and flying from there with www.airfrance.com because with various former French colonies on the continent, travelling there is more common.

Although flights to Africa can be long as you are going down instead of across the world, the time change is only a few hours so you will not suffer from much jet lag.

The best way to travel depends on your whereabouts and how far you want to go. Away from the main tourist areas and large cities, a lot of the roads are very poor so if you want to drive independently, you need to plan your route carefully. There are buses available but the rides can be a bit rocky and often overcrowded so aren't advised, although South Africa does have a good bus network. See www.bazbus.com.

If you going any distance then you should consider getting a flight or joining an organised tour. Both can be pricey and tours can feel limiting but they are sometimes the best way to visit more remote areas.

'Although flights to Africa can be long as you are going down instead of across the world, the time change is only a few hours so you will not suffer from much jet lag.'

Health and safety

Unfortunately, Africa is one of the worst continents for both disease and political unrest. This should not put you off visiting but you must make sure that you get all the correct vaccinations and check with the foreign office before travelling. Hepatitis A and B, boosters of tetanus, measles and polio, meningococcal meningitis, typhoid and yellow fever vaccinations are all recommended. As well as vaccinations, you will need to take malaria tablets for most countries on the continent. Sub Saharan Africa has the highest HIV rate in the world, so you also need to be particularly vigilant about practising safe sex.

Africa can still be a dangerous and unwelcoming place if you end up in the wrong place, so always be sensible about where you travel to. It is important to remain vigilant and, unless you are sticking to the main tourist centres, it is not the best place to travel alone, especially if you are a woman.

Costs

Although flights to Africa can be quite expensive, once you get there costs are generally cheap. Basic living costs would be around £5-15 per day unless you are visiting places such as Cape Town, Botswana and Namibia where this can rise drastically. Obviously though, it depends on what you want to do. There are some amazing locations to stay in and one of the most popular things to do in Africa is to go on safari. You can do variations of this on a budget but it is still going to be quite expensive and something that you should budget for in advance.

Haggling is the done thing in Africa and you will be expected to barter for your goods. Always start at a price much lower than you are willing to pay. This can feel a bit overwhelming at first, especially if the stall owners are being particularly pushy. Only do what you are comfortable with and if the situation feels aggressive then walk away.

Africa isn't as well set up for the backpacker as more popular destinations such as Asia, so outside the main hubs, hostels and low cost accommodation can be of a varying standard. You can get some really cheap, tasty food across the continent, and even in big cities like Cape Town the restaurants are still great value.

Living and working

Unless you have organised a specific job in advance, Africa is not an easy place to live and work. It is a popular destination for volunteer work but make sure you know what the living conditions are like and be prepared to face up to scenes of poverty.

Africa is also popular for tour guide work as there is so much call for safaris and organised trips. Companies have different requirements but will usually need you to have travelled extensively in the area and been on their tours. There are some specific training schemes available but make sure you sign up with a reputable company and are given the support and training that you need.

Action points

- Be sure you have the correct vaccinations and malaria tablets.
- Check with the foreign office for areas of unrest.
- If you want to go on safari, make sure you have budgeted for it in advance.
- If you are volunteering, be clear about what you are signing up for.
- Plan your travel in advance.

Summing Up

Africa is an infectious place that will get under your skin. Don't be put off by its image but do be sensible about where you travel and how you get there. It is also important that you have the correct vaccinations to stay healthy. Whether you want to play it safe and enjoy the great city of Cape Town or are ready to explore further into the continent, be ready for some culture shock.

- Watch: *Long Way Down* with Ewan McGregor and Charley Boorman.
- Read: *Out of Africa* by Karen Blixen.
- Surf: www.africaguide.com.

Chapter Eight

North America

They are our allies and the provider of many of our TV shows, but there is still something oddly alluring about North America. With its big ideals, big roads and even bigger meals, everything is turned up a notch or two in the 'land of plenty'.

Where to go

If you are looking for the high life then fly into LA, hire a car and drive up the coast to San Francisco and over to Las Vegas, taking in the Grand Canyon on your way. Or for east coast cool, start off in New York, pop to Washington for some political culture and fly down to Miami to party. To see more of the 'real' America, jump on a bus and cruise down the iconic Route 66 or head south and experience the charms of New Orleans and Louisiana. Don't forget Canada though! A trip coast to coast by plane, train or automobile takes you through some stunning scenery. Get a taste for the outdoors by taking a trip out into the vast wilderness, have a European moment in Quebec and end up in Vancouver for the perfect mix of the city and outdoors lifestyle.

> 'The most riveting thing about New York is that anything can happen there.'
> Bill Bryson.

What to see

New York City, New York

It's the city that never sleeps because there's so much to see and do – climb the empire state building, explore central park or take a trip across the Hudson River.

LA Walk of Fame, California

Yes, it's tacky but while you are in LA, try to find the handprints of your favourite star – or you may even spot the real thing!

Grand Canyon, Arizona

This vast expanse is breathtaking and if you can afford a helicopter ride over the top, it will blow you away.

Las Vegas, Nevada

Whether you enjoy gambling or not, you can't help but be amazed by the attitude of this city and the size of everything they have on offer.

Niagara Falls, Ontario, Canada

It may be surrounded by tacky, flashy attractions but donning the plastic poncho and taking to the water is still worth the trip.

What to do

Take a road trip

North America is vast and the best way to see it is to get out on the open road and stop off at all the random places along the way.

Shop on Fifth Avenue

OK, so it may just be window shopping but wandering down Fifth Avenue is a classic New York experience.

Gamble in Las Vegas

You don't have to be a high roller to enjoy a few free drinks and soak up the atmosphere of the most famous casinos in the world.

Go to a rodeo

Could you get anything much more American? Yeeeehaaah! Ride 'em cowboy!

Have pancakes

If the Americans know how to do one thing, it's make a good meal. Find some space to indulge in a sumptuous breakfast.

Customs, laws and language

Although it may seem that England is just an extension of America, you will be surprised to see how different their attitudes and customs can be. At least you have a leg up on the language – well, once you master your elevators, eggplants, sidewalks, zucchinis and SUVs. North America is so vast, with the state of Texas alone being larger than the UK, that there is great diversity. The people that you meet in New York are a world away from those in Kansas and it is this mix that makes it such an interesting country.

Remember that you cannot drink until you are 21 in America, which can be a bit of a shock to the system. They are very strict about asking for ID, so you should always carry some with you. If you don't have it on you, it is unlikely that you will get served anywhere.

Canada, which is often forgotten next to its loud, brash neighbour, has more English influence and is more reserved. Quebec is French speaking and has a very European vibe about it, although in most areas, especially the main cities, you will be able to get by speaking English.

'With its big ideals, big roads and even bigger meals everything is turned up a notch or two in the land of plenty.'

Getting there and getting around

Flights to North America are relatively cheap and can usually be bought as part of a round-the-world ticket. They don't have the same cheap flight culture that we do, so flights within the country can work out a bit pricey. There are many bus networks such as www.greyhound.com which are the cheapest way to travel, but remember it is a long way between major cities. Their trains are expensive and not that extensive, unless you are on the east coast.

Another option, and the best way to see the country, is to hire a car, but you will need to be over 25. One way to do it is to use a company that transports people's personal cars for them if they need them moved across the country but don't want to do the drive. The company will assign you a specific car and destination and although you will have to cover the petrol costs and be expected to arrive in a certain amount of time, the car use is free. Visit www.autodriveaway.com.

Health and safety

Generally, North America is a safe place to travel around although you need to be careful in the major cities, just like anywhere in the world. Beware of pickpockets, keep your wits about you and make sure you don't end up in a cheaper area of the city just to save a few pounds.

If you are going to travel to more remote areas, especially in sparsely populated regions of Canada, then you need to make sure you are prepared. Have the correct equipment and make sure that you tell someone where you are planning to go. For more extreme expeditions, it is best to go on an organised trip.

Costs

The cost of living is generally cheaper in North America than the UK, but it really depends on the fluctuating exchange rate just how much of a bargain you get. Clothes and eating out are particularly good value although travel tends to work out a bit more. You can get by on around £20 per day but it will vary greatly depending on whether you are in a big city or a rural outpost. If you

Need2Know

want to take up some activities or travel remotely in Canada, you will need to boost your budget.

Even in the big cities across North America you can still find some budget backpacker accommodation and motels en route can be a bargain. Even though fast food, which the continent is famous for, often doesn't work out as the cheapest option, eating out is still much cheaper than in the UK.

Tipping is big in America and you will be expected to add on 15-20% in a restaurant, although sometimes this is done automatically. You will also be expected to tip taxi drivers and leave an extra dollar or two when you buy a round of drinks, which can soon add up.

Working and living

The USA is quite strict about handing out working visas but if you are a student or are being sponsored by a company or work programme, then there are lots of opportunities. It is a great place to live and work because language is not a problem. There are vast differences in different areas of the country and the attitude to working life in New York is poles apart from Kansas.

There is some interesting seasonal work available in North America and a popular option is working at a summer camp such as www.campamerica. co.uk. These can be quite claustrophobic as you are looking after children for up to 12 weeks but they are also a lot of fun and allow time for travel. Another big draw are the internships which are huge in the US and also in Canada. Getting a placement at a large respected company will give you invaluable international experience and look great on your CV. Visit www.bunac.org.

Action points

- Expect to spend more than you would in poorer areas of the world.
- Make sure that you have the correct visa for visiting or working.
- Remember to tip staff in restaurants and bars.
- Consider combining your trip with some seasonal work or an internship.
- Don't forget Canada!

'Even though fast food, which the continent is famous for, often doesn't work out as the cheapest option, eating out is still much cheaper than in the UK.'

Summing Up

It may not be the most exotic of gap year destinations but there is still plenty to see and learn in North America. The cities are bigger and brasher than ours and the small towns more remote and conservative. Road tripping is the best way to see the USA although the east coast is fairly compact for rail or bus travel. Don't strike Canada off the list as it has some great cities (Vancouver and Quebec) and some outstanding scenery, especially if you love to be outdoors.

- Watch: *Stephen Fry: In America*.
- Read: *On The Road* by Jack Kerouac.
- Surf: www.roadtripusa.com.

Chapter Nine

Latin America

South America is full of passion and soul. Its array of landscapes will astound you, but it is the people that make you want to go back for more. Stretching from Mexico all the way down to the Antarctic, there is a lot to take in. You could spend your whole gap year just on this one continent.

Where to go

Probably the most popular route in South America, nicknamed the 'gringo trail', is Peru, Bolivia then Ecuador. Marvel at the Bolivian salt flats before bussing it to Cusco and splashing out on a trip to the jungle or the Galapagos Islands, but leave some time to step off the tourist trail and meet the locals too. For party people, Brazil and Argentina are the places to go. Start in Rio and take in the amazing Iguazu Falls before stopping in Buenos Aires. Continue your trip by going south to the enchanting Patagonia or across to Chile. Central America should also not be forgotten. Get your sun, sea and margarita fix on the coast of Mexico before balancing it with some culture by visiting the Mayan ruins. For the eco friendly, Costa Rica is the place to go or enjoy the sea life of the Caribbean.

What to see

Machu Picchu, Peru

Often referred to as the lost city of the Inca's, this ancient site, set on top of a mountain, is one of those places that you feel won't live up to all its hype – but it does.

'Get up there before the rush of tourists and you can feel like you are alone in the ruins – for half an hour or so at least.'

Chris, talking about Machu Picchu.

Bolivian Salt Flats

It takes a while to really believe that this massive landscape of salt from dried up lakes is not ice and then a while longer to take in this crazy feat of nature.

Amazon rainforest

Home to some of the most isolated tribes in the world, South America isn't complete without a journey into the jungle.

Galapagos Islands, Ecuador

If you are a wildlife lover then a trip to these islands is a must, especially for the turtles.

Rio De Janeiro, Brazil

One of the most flamboyant cities in the world, Rio does everything to the extreme.

Things to do

Learn Spanish

With so many countries to choose from, you will soon be able to say more than just 'beer please'.

Take a tango lesson

Even if you can't speak like a South American, you can move like one by perfecting your dance moves.

Walk the Inca trail

It is a challenging and tiring trip but the pain will all be worthwhile when you see the sunrise over Machu Picchu.

Go to Rio carnival

It's the ultimate place to let loose, so drink, dance and be merry at this party of all parties.

Enjoy a margarita

Sitting by the pool sipping a margarita is the epitome of a luxury beach break, but in Mexico it doesn't need to break the bank.

Customs, laws and language

The majority of central and Southern America speak Spanish, while the odd ones out are the Brazilians who speak Portuguese instead. In the main tourist traps you will find that you can get by with English but if you are going off the beaten track, it is a good idea to brush up on your Spanish skills you learnt at school!

The South Americans are often known for their friendly and welcoming demeanour and this is generally true, although female travellers should be cautious and take extra care, especially if travelling alone.

While the whole of the continent is friendly, there is quite a difference between the more traditional communities where family and customs are important and the eclectic mix of the big cities like Rio. Be prepared to adjust your behaviour accordingly depending on the areas that you are heading for.

'Try and embrace the local culture by visiting markets, going salsa dancing and trying out your Spanish – however limited!'

Getting there and getting around

Flights to South America can often be included on a round-the-world ticket but flying directly there can be quite pricey. Within the continent, flights are still quite expensive, so overland travel, especially by bus, is very popular. Although the journeys can be very long, the network is well set up, with many companies serving meals and even playing bingo en route. In some cases, because of the terrain or sheer distance, it may be worth splashing out on an internal flight.

South America does not have a vast rail network apart from a few limited routes and tourist services. It is possible to hire a car but the distances are vast. There are many organised tours across South America which are a good idea if you don't have much time, would like the expertise of a guide or are visiting places you can't go without one such as the Inca trail. Visit www.incatrailperu.com for more information.

'There are many organised tours across South America which are a good idea if you don't have much time, would like the expertise of a guide or are visiting places you can't go without one.'

Health and safety

It is a good idea to check the political situation before travelling to some countries in South America – Colombia is especially unstable. The Darien gap, which connects central and South America, is the scene of numerous robberies and kidnappings and is definitely worth paying the airfare to avoid.

Health wise, you need to be careful about drinking the water in many countries and if you are visiting tropical areas be sure you have all the necessary vaccinations. Recommended ones are hepatitis A and B, rabies, typhoid, yellow fever and boosters for tetanus and measles. If you are visiting Machu Picchu or other mountainous areas, you are likely to suffer from some altitude sickness.

South America is generally not a dangerous place but some people will try their luck and attempt to scam you. Be careful not to mark yourself out as a tourist and leave valuables well hidden.

Costs

South America is generally fairly budget friendly but it all depends on where you are visiting. Peru, Bolivia and Ecuador are particularly cheap and you can live comfortably on £10 per day. Argentina, Brazil and Chile are a bit pricier but you should still be fine on £15-20 per day. If you would like to do any big trips such as visiting the jungle, going to the Galapagos Islands or hiking the Inca trail then budget for this in advance and shop around for the best deals – which can often be found locally.

There is a huge network of hostels across the continent and it is good to gather recommendations as you go. Home stays are also popular and can be a great way to save money and get to know the locals. You can buy some great food from the local markets but basic fare in local restaurants is also a cheap option. Haggling is normal in this area of the world but is not as aggressive as in Africa and they will stop when they reach a price they are not happy with. Travelling around South America is generally quite cheap but activities and accommodation on the 'gringo trail' can be overpriced so it is worth shopping around.

Living and working

South America is a popular destination for language courses such as www. linguaschools.com which are often combined with a stint of volunteering. The South Americans are very friendly and family orientated and lots of these courses will be combined with a home stay. Don't expect the same standards of décor and luxury that you are used to at home but you will always be well looked after, treated as part of the family and fed regularly. Try to embrace the local culture by visiting markets, going salsa dancing and trying out your Spanish – however limited!

Action points

- Learn some Spanish before you go.
- Be prepared for some long bus rides.

- Devote enough time to really see this exuberant continent.
- Make sure you have the correct vaccines – especially for tropical areas.
- Avoid more dangerous areas such as the Darien gap.

Summing Up

South America is a continent packed with fun. There are some amazing things to see and do but also some great people to meet. The gringo trail has developed for a reason as it takes you through some of the top places, but to get a real sense of places try and divert at least a little bit. It is easy to get around by bus and you can live on quite a small budget unless you want to party in the big cities or enjoy the resorts on the beaches of Mexico.

- Watch: *The Motorcycle Diaries* directed by Walter Salles.
- Read: *In Patagonia* by Bruce Chatwun.
- Surf: www.saexplorers.org.

'South America is a continent packed with fun. There are some amazing things to see and do but also some great people to meet.'

Chapter Ten

Australia, New Zealand and the Pacific

Australia is traditionally the most popular gap year destination as it has always been easy to get a working visa. It offers a chance to enjoy the sun, sea and sand while earning some money along the way. Hang out in the backpacking haunts of Sydney, get down with nature at the Great Barrier Reef or experience the vast nothingness of the outback – Australia is so much more than beer and barbecues!

However, you must not forget about New Zealand and the Pacific Islands as both offer some truly stunning destinations. The idyllic islands of Fiji and Tahiti and the wide landscapes of New Zealand lure visitors into never wanting to leave.

'God bless America. God Save the Queen. God defend New Zealand and thank Christ for Australia.'

Russel Crowe.

Where to go

The east coast of Australia is the most popular destination and takes in Sydney, where you will probably fly into, Melbourne and the Great Barrier Reef. It's a shame to miss out on the middle though, so circle up past Ayres Rock and Alice Springs if you have the time. Western Australia is very remote which is good if you like that sort of thing but can take a lot out of your journey, so think about whether it is worth it. New Zealand is split into the North Island, where Auckland is, and the South Island, home to Milford Sound. Both are worth a visit and are home to some amazing scenery and a whole host of outdoor activities. It would be a mistake to travel this far round the world without taking in one of the Pacific Islands. Take your pick and remember that some of the less well known ones can give a cheaper and more authentic experience.

What to see

Sydney Opera House

This performing arts centre is one of the 20th century's most distinctive buildings and is at the heart of the city with great views of the harbour and bridge.

Great Barrier Reef

If you think that little dots of sand with a palm tree in the middle are only real on postcards, then you need to come here to see the real thing.

Ayres Rock

You have to travel a long way to see it but this feat of nature is a symbol of the size and scale of Australia.

Bondi beach

Famous for its surfing, this is one of the most popular destinations for young backpackers – many would say this is what Australia is all about.

Milford Sound, New Zealand

This amazing fjord, set in a national park, is New Zealand's most popular destination, great for adrenalin junkies and nature lovers alike.

Things to do

Go diving

If you love to dive then there is nowhere better than the Great Barrier Reef. If you can't dive, here is a great place to learn!

Have a barbecue on the beach

Join in the Aussie culture and get down to the beach for a beer and some al fresco dining.

Climb Sydney Harbour Bridge

There is no better place to view Sydney than from on top of the famous Harbour Bridge.

Cuddle a Koala

Make sure you do this in a zoo or animal park as Koalas in the wild can be quite vicious, but captive, they are awfully cute!!

Start surfing

You can't go to Australia and not go surfing, so sign up for a lesson and learn how to catch those waves without making a fool of yourself!

Customs, laws and language

Australians are famed for their laid back attitude and will soon be inviting you to a barbecue on the beach. Although they technically speak English, there are a lot of variations, but you will soon pick up on the local slang.

'There is no better place to view Sydney than from on top of the famous Harbour Bridge.'

New Zealand has a great mix of cultures originating from many European countries and they all share a great love for the outdoors.

People of the South Pacific Islands are very friendly and welcoming. These remote destinations have their own language and ingrained culture where family and tradition are important. French is widely spoken but you should be able to get by speaking English most of the time.

Getting there and getting around

'Australia is the eternal backpacker haven and has earned its reputation for its easy working visas, safe environment, stunning scenery and outgoing people.'

Australia and the South Pacific is a long way away from England! You haven't got much choice but to fly there unless you fancy a very long boat trip. The best way to visit is by buying a round-the-world flight. These usually don't work out much more than buying a standard return but allow you to stop off in a number of places on the way.

Australia is vast and it takes a long time to travel from one place to the next, especially if you want to visit central or western Australia. Travelling up and down the east coast can be done by hiring a car. Another popular choice is to buy a camper van. Alternatively, there are lots of bus companies that you can join to take you around such as www.ozexperience.com, and the same applies in New Zealand. If you have limited time then you should consider investing in a few internal flights.

The islands of the South Pacific are always an option on round-the-world flights and it is well worth adding one on as getting there independently can be very expensive.

Health and safety

Another reason why Australia and New Zealand are popular gap year destinations is because they are relatively safe and with few health risks. Sharks and poisonous spiders are dangerous but the biggest risk is the scorching sun, so make sure you cover up and use a high factor sun cream while you are out and about.

Need2Know

If you are going further afield than mainland Australia and New Zealand, it is worth getting vaccinated against tetanus, hepatitis A and B, typhoid and measles.

Tahiti has one of the lowest crime rates in the world, so you can generally expect to be safe when you travel around this region of the world. However, make sure you tell someone if you are planning to go off into the more remote areas and ensure that you have plenty of water and supplies.

Costs

While the cost of living in Australia is generally much cheaper than the UK, you are not going to get by as cheaply as travelling in Asia or South America. Although petrol is much cheaper, travelling around can be costly because of the large distances that you cover. You can expect to get by on around £15-19 a day but, as you will probably stop off and work somewhere along the way, your costs will vary and you will have a chance to save up.

There are many hostels in Australia and the climate is good for camping, although the popular option of buying a campervan can be a budget friendly way to travel and sleep.

If you want to visit Tahiti, expect to pay out a lot more. Although other islands such as The Cook Islands can be a good cheaper alternative, you still need to expect to push your budget.

Living and working

Australia is a very popular place for Brits to go and work because it is easy to get a working holiday visa (see www.immi.gov.au/visitors/working-holiday). There is a lot of work available but there are restrictions on the type of work that you can do and for how long.

You will generally find it easy to find somewhere to live as there is a huge British expat community and many temporary visitors. You will never feel too far from home but it can be a good idea to try not to rely on this – make friends with the locals instead.

The Pacific Islands are popular for environmental volunteering and you can be working in some idyllic locations, although these types of trips can be a bit pricey.

Action points

- Include the Pacific Islands on a round-the-world flight.

- Factor in enough time to earn some money.

- Don't get caught up in the expat community – meet the locals.

- Get active in New Zealand.

- Wear sunscreen.

Summing Up

Australia is the eternal backpacker haven and has earned its reputation for its easy working visas, safe environment, stunning scenery and outgoing people. While you are in this corner of the world, try to fit in a visit to New Zealand which is a great destination for adrenalin junkies and nature enthusiasts. The islands of the South Pacific are also definitely worth a stop as they are paradise on earth!

- Watch: *Australia* directed by Baz Luhrmann.
- Read: *Down Under* by Bill Bryson.
- Surf: www.bugpacific.com.

Chapter Eleven

Europe

Most people will have visited Europe when they were growing up, so it doesn't seem as exotic as far-flung destinations. However, by stepping from one country to the next, it is easy to experience a huge variety of culture, language and scenery without ever changing currency or showing your passport. History, food and architecture are on show around every corner, and east and west offer very different experiences.

Where to go

Western Europe may not seem very exotic but it has a lot to offer and is easy to navigate by train, car or cheap flight networks. Start in the romantic heart of Paris before heading south to Spain and indulging in the variety that this vast country has to offer. Make like a movie star and cross through the south of France before heading down to Italy and ferry hopping over to the Greek islands. If that's all old hat to you then explore Eastern Europe. Croatia with its stunning coastline is a good place to start and then take a look at Bosnia, Serbia and Romania which are much more than ex-war torn countries. Bulgaria is also a great budget choice. If you are not drawn by the sun and sea then the Baltic countries are something a bit different. Fly into Tallinn, take the ferry over to Finland (or start in the hedonistic Amsterdam) and head up through Copenhagen and onto Sweden for some clean living. Further afield, Russia is an interesting trip. Fly to Moscow or St Petersburg to whet your appetite or consider an organised trip if you want to go further afield.

'The great thing about Europe is that you can experience so many different languages and cultures in a short space of time.'

What to see

Eiffel Tower, France

It's a classic and always will be. Whether you are with a lover or on your own, there is still a sense of romance about this famous attraction.

Colosseum, Italy

It is amazing to think how long this Roman amphitheatre has been standing for – imagine the gladiatorial games that it was once home to.

Northern Lights

There's nothing else like this natural phenomenon, so head to northern Scandinavia between September and April for the chance to marvel at it.

Sistine Chapel, Italy

Classy and classic, you'll be blown away that Michaelangelo painted this ceiling upside down.

The Kremlin, Russia

A fascinating insight into Russia, this fortified governmental building sits at the heart of Moscow.

Things to do

Take a gondola ride in Venice

Join the other tourists and jump on a gondola. It is a great way to see another view of the city and you might even get sung to!

Go skiing

Whether you are a beginner or a pro, it's always an adrenalin kick and a chance to see some amazing scenery.

Have a sauna in the snow

Such a Scandinavian thing to do, this experience is fun, exhilarating and great for the skin!

Greek island hopping

The stunning beaches and picture perfect villages are all just a short ferry trip away.

Soak up the culture

Art, music, fashion and food – Europe has it all on offer round every corner, so seek it out and soak it up.

'The Europe I saw on my gap year was not the same English-centric place I remember as a kid. It's a shame so many people overlook it for far-flung destinations.'

Amy, 23.

Customs, laws and language

The great thing about Europe is that you can experience so many different languages and cultures in a short space of time. Most people have studied French or Spanish at school, so you should be able to get by with the basic phrases in Western Europe, although Eastern Europe and Scandinavia are a different matter.

The English have got a bit of a reputation in Europe for being 'Brits abroad' and you may find in some places they try to take advantage of this. However, as long as you are friendly and respectful then you can expect a warm welcome in most places as the Europeans are very family orientated.

In Germany and some Eastern European countries, people can come across as a bit rude and abrupt. Don't be put off by this as they are perfectly friendly and it is just a cultural difference. Scandinavians are often very outgoing and welcoming and love to have a good time.

'Over the last few years, the cheap flight market has exploded, meaning that it has never cost less to fly to Europe.'

Getting there and getting around

Over the last few years, the cheap flight market has exploded, meaning that it has never cost less to fly to Europe. A great bonus of this is that you can buy single flights instead of returns as you are unlikely to want to fly home from the same airport. Just check which airports they fly into as often they can be so far away from your intended destination that you pay just as much again on taxis into the city.

For the eco-conscious, travelling by train is a great way to see Europe. Rail passes can be the most economical choice as they give you unlimited travel within your chosen countries. You can buy them online at www.raileurope.com or in person at stations across Europe. The train system on the continent is extensive, reliable and a relatively cheap way of getting around. Another option is to drive which gives you flexibility but, with the price of petrol, may not be the cheapest way to do it.

Health and safety

Generally, Europe is quite a safe place to travel in and is free from lots of the worst diseases and political problems. However, it is recommended that you have an up-to-date tetanus shot and, if you are travelling to many Eastern European countries, it is suggested that you have the hepatitis A vaccination too.

In the major cities, you can be vulnerable to pickpockets and muggings. Like any city, stay away form the less desirable areas and don't have your valuables on display. The metros can be the worst places for pickpockets so never leave things in easy-to-reach pockets and turn your bags around so they can't get into them without you noticing.

Costs

Since the majority of Europe has now signed up to the Euro, it has become more expensive to visit many countries. Eastern Europe is still great value but if you want to stay in Italy or France, it will cost you almost as much as in the UK. Expect to budget about £25 a day in Western Europe if you stay in hostels and eat cheaply. In some areas of Eastern Europe, you can still get by on as little as £10-15 a day.

Europe's markets are a great place to pick up fresh fruit and vegetables at bargain prices and if you pick the restaurants that the locals visit, you can still get some very reasonably priced meals – often with a glass of wine thrown in! Accommodation in the main cities isn't all that cheap, but if you travel over to Eastern Europe you can stay in some good hotels for less.

Living and working

Because of the EU it is easy to go and work in many European countries. There is a lot of seasonal work to pick up either in the holiday industry or in agriculture and it is easy to go over there for a few months. If your language skills are good, you may decide to stay for longer and settle into a more permanent job. Check out www.eurojobs.com.

Europe is a popular place to study or take language classes and it is a great way to soak up the culture. Studying at university for a year is often possible as part of a university course and this can be an ideal way to integrate into the country. There are often a lot of expat communities, especially in the major cities, but you will pick up the lingo a lot quicker if you force yourself to speak it every day and mix with the locals.

Although it used to be quite cheap to live in Europe, the Euro exchange rate means that you will find many places are not much cheaper than living in the UK.

Action points

- Protect your valuables from pickpockets on the metro.
- Check which airport your cheap flight arrives at.
- Brush up on your language skills.
- Go to Eastern Europe with no preconceptions.
- Budget more while the Euro rate is poor.

Summing Up

People from across the world flock to Europe every year and just because it is on your doorstep you shouldn't rule it out as a worthy gap year destination. Western Europe has a lot to offer in terms of culture and scenery. However, if you want something a bit different, Eastern Europe and Russia are the places to visit. Also, don't forget about Scandinavia which can give you a new perspective on the best way to live and a fresh attitude to life.

- Watch: *Before Sunrise* directed by Richard Linklater.
- Read: *A Year in Provence* by Peter Mayle.
- Surf: www.guideforeurope.com.

Chapter Twelve

Re-adjustment

When you are on your gap year, every day is filled with new, exciting experiences that are a world away from your old life at home. At some point though, you are going to have to return to reality and leave your travels behind. Although you may have missed your friends and family, getting back home always ends up being an anti-climax. Life has stayed the same, there is nothing exciting to do and nobody seems interested enough in all your adventures. It can take time to settle back down again but knowing you will have these feelings, and taking constructive steps to deal with them, can make the transition a little bit easier.

Staying in touch

Staying in touch on your travels not only lets your friends and family know that you are safe, it also allows you to share your adventures and maintain a relationship with them while you are away.

It can be difficult to keep regular contact with everyone but the wonders of modern technology make it a lot easier. Even the remotest outposts now have Internet connection, although a quick phone call will always be welcomed by your nearest and dearest.

Skype

Skype is a great invention that means you can make phone calls through the Internet. All you need to do is sign up and get yourself a headset, then it is free to make and receive calls. You will both have to be online in order for it to work, so you will need to arrange a day and time in advance.

Phones

Making calls from a UK mobile can be very costly, so find out about the charges beforehand. If you are staying in a country for any length of time, it can be worth buying a cheap local mobile. Don't forget about phone cards though. These are usually much cheaper, can be picked up easily and used on any payphone.

Email and instant messenger

If your parents are not very technically savvy, give them a crash course in email and instant messenger. It is easy to use and is the most convenient way to stay in touch. While group emails are a good way to keep friends and family up-to-date, taking the extra time to reply individually will always be appreciated.

Blogs and social networking

We are used to reading about the ins and outs of people's everyday lives on the Internet, and sharing your news on-mass is considered normal. By setting up a blog or posting on sites such as Facebook, you can create an interactive way to communicate with your friends. This can also be a great way to record your travels to look back on when you return.

Down in the dumps

It is only natural that when you get home from your gap year you will feel down. You have just had an amazing time and coming back to the boredom of everyday life is going to be a let down. Your perspective on life is likely to have changed and your old town, friends and life may seem uninspiring.

Remember that just because you are home, it doesn't mean the fun has ended. Now is the time to start looking towards the future and planning your next adventure. Instead of seeing your friends and family as boring, spend time with them, fill them in on your adventure and catch up on what they have been doing.

If you are feeling low, go for a walk, look at your photos or start researching your next step. The best thing you can do is focus on all the great things that are to come instead of what you have left behind.

How can you preserve your memories?

Your year has no doubt been packed with lifelong memories that you will still be talking about to your grandchildren. It is natural that you will want to preserve these as much as possible. Photos are a great way to keep memories alive but so often they just languish on the computer. Make the effort to buy some photo albums and print off your favourites. This will be a great way of reliving your experiences and sharing them with others.

While you were away you may have kept a diary or journal. This is a lovely thing to look back on when you are older, so take good care of it. Perhaps you could make it into a scrapbook or add to your thoughts now you are back. If you kept an electronic diary or blog, consider printing it out so that you have a tangible piece of writing that you can store away for the future.

Also, along the way, you are bound to have made many friends from across the world. With technology, it is so easy to keep in touch with people that you must make sure you do so. Then, the next time that you get itchy feet you will have someone to stay with!

'I never travel without my diary. One should always have something sensational to read in the train.'
Oscar Wilde.

Itchy feet

However many amazing places you see, there will always be more that you want to visit. When you arrive home from your gap year you will probably be planning your next adventure, spurred on by other travellers you have met along the way.

Having this feeling means that it can be difficult to settle down, so you need to plan some trips to keep you satisfied. Even if it is just within the UK to visit friends or to go to a new city, it will give you something to focus on.

Get a globe, buy some guide books or go to the library and start thinking about your next adventure. Even if you don't have the time or funds to do it any time soon, it gives you something to fill that void.

Dealing with a change of perspective

When you travel you will see and experience so many new things and meet people from all different cultures and backgrounds. It can really open your eyes to the world and leave you with a fresh perspective and a new set of opinions.

This new perspective can make it difficult to fit back in with your old set of friends and can lead you to question the beliefs of your family. It is good that you have discovered more about the world but don't judge everyone by your new view. Inflicting your views on your friends and family will only alienate you. Instead, think about how you can use them constructively.

Consider reading up on the things you have learnt or taking a course that suits your new outlook on life. Start planning another trip so that you can go back to the place that inspired you, or put your experience to good use in a volunteer project. Another important thing to think about is choosing a career path that fits in with your new view with the world. However, remember while you feel strongly about these things now, your commitment may fade over time, so don't blow off your current plans until you are sure.

How do you settle into university?

If you have taken your gap year before you go to university, it can be tricky settling back down to study.

If you look back at the person you were before you went on your gap year, you probably feel very different now. Travelling and spending time away from home helps you grow up and gives you a new perspective on the world.

One thing you may find is that your peers seem a lot younger than you. Although it will only be by one year, having come straight from home, they will not be as worldly wise.

The thing to remember is that there are so many people to meet at university that you are guaranteed to find someone who has the same outlook as you. Try not to look down upon other students who have not taken time out – look for common ground that you can enjoy together.

'When you travel you will see and experience so many new things and meet people from all different cultures and backgrounds. It can really open your eyes to the world and leave you with a fresh perspective and a new set of opinions.'

Instead of constantly looking back at your gap year and being unable to settle, focus your energies on making the most of this new experience and embracing university life.

Finding a job

When you return from your gap year, the reality of everyday life can hit you hard. Whether you have left education and need to get started on your career, or just need some part-time work to pay off debts or see you through college, it can be a daunting prospect. Okay, working is not going to be as exciting as travelling the world, but there is a lot to look forward to. You can use your new experiences, outlook on the world and time away to help you find the job you want.

Modern employers, far from looking down on gap years, now realise that they produce more well rounded and confident employees. What you need to do is emphasise what you have learnt from your experiences and how these translate into skills you can use for employment. Ask yourself:

- What do I enjoy doing?
- What am I good at?
- What am I interested in?
- How can I adapt my skills to the workplace?
- How can I illustrate my experience with examples?

Once you have thought up the answers to these questions, compose a CV that shows what you have learnt and the skills that you have gained. Try to use solid examples in interviews of times that have been challenging or where you have been forced to think up a new solution or work well with others.

Fitting back into your career

If you are a bit older and took a career break, the thought of going back to the everyday grind can make you want to run for the hills.

You may find that your gap year has given you new focus and drive and reaffirmed how you feel about your career. However, you may find that you have been left questioning a lot of the things that you took for granted before your trip.

Don't make any rash decisions, return to your job and take time to process all your feelings before you act on them. See if there is any way of adapting your current job or grasping opportunities within the company.

If not, do your research to find out what else is out there and what you would need to do to make the transition. It is great that you are inspired but think carefully about how you will feel in a year's time when you come down off your gap year high, and whether you are willing to commit to long term changes.

Looking to the future

When you have taken a gap year and had a life changing trip, it can be easy to keep looking back and reminiscing about all the experiences you had. There is nothing wrong with this, of course you want to remember the fun times, but you also need to focus on the future.

You may already have something that you are coming back to, such as an old job or a place at university, and if so, you need to make the most of it. Share your travels with your friends but make sure you work hard at fitting into your new reality.

If you have no firm plans then now is the time to make some. Think about what you would like to be doing this time next year and start figuring out how to make that happen. Yes, you have had an amazing year but there are many more to come and you don't want to be that person that spends their whole life talking about one year. Instead, fill your life with lots of amazing years.

'When you arrive home from your gap year you will probably be planning your next adventure, spurred on by other travellers you have met along the way.'

Action points

- Stay in touch with family and friends, and make an effort to catch up with them when you get back.

- Be prepared to feel low and frustrated when you get back.

- Make a scrap book, print off your photos and preserve your journal.

- Take time to think about what you want to do next and take practical steps to make the changes.

Reflection form

What was your favourite country and why?

Where did you feel most inspired?

Describe the most interesting person you met on your trip.

What were your top three sights?

1.

2.

3.

Describe your favourite day of the trip.

What has your gap year taught you about yourself?

How has it changed you?

Give an example of when you:

… had to think on your feet.

… faced a new situation.

… worked with people from other cultures.

… were put outside your comfort zone.

What practical skills have you learnt?

How has it changed your perspective on the world?

Summing Up

Arriving back home to your old life can make you feel like the walls are closing in around you. However, far from being the end of your adventures, it is only the beginning. Now you know what you are capable of and what the world has to offer, you can start looking towards an exciting future. Whether it is embracing university, changing career or planning your next travels, start taking practical steps towards achieving it. Try not to dwell on what you have left behind but preserve your memories so you can always look back and remember the great times you had.

Help List

When you've got the whole world to research it can be difficult to know where to start. Here is a list of useful websites and organisations that can help you on your way.

Flights

Airtreks

www.airtreks.com
This site is a good place for round-the-world flights and also has a useful 'planning your trip' tool.

Expedia

www.expedia.com
Expedia is an extensive travel portal which is useful for booking flights, hotels or car hire and comparing what's on offer.

Round The World Flights

www.roundtheworldflights.com
Tel: 0207 704 5700
An easy-to-use website that allows you to design your own round-the world-flight. Great for getting ideas and comparing different routes and prices but if you need some help, you can always give them a call.

Skyscanner

www.skyscanner.net
This travel portal concentrates on budget airlines, so it is a really good tool for finding cheap flights across Europe.

STA Travel

www.statravel.co.uk
Tel: 0871 230 0040
STA are specialists in student and gap year travel. They can offer some good discounts and worldwide advice.

Trailfinders

www.trailfinders.com
Tel: 0845 058 5858 (worldwide flights)
0845 054 6060 (tailormade trips)
Trailfinders are well known for their tailormade travel packages and, with their extensive knowledge and enthusiasm, can help you organise the trip that you are looking for.

Other travel

CrewSeekers International

www.crewseekers.net
Find out all you need to know about working on a yacht and search out yacht owners who are currently seeking staff.

Freighter World Cruises, Inc

www.freighterworld.com
info@freighterworld.com
Find out about the different routes available on freighter ships, what to expect and how to book your journey.

Rail-Europe

www.raileurope.co.uk
The one-stop-shop for finding out everything about rail travel across Europe, from timetables to tickets and routes.

Money

International Student Travel Confederation

www.istc.org
This is the place to get yourself an international student card which can give you access to a host of discounts across the world.

Moneygram

www.moneygram.com
Moneygram allows you to transfer money across 190 countries, so it's the perfect back up if you find yourself stranded.

XE

www.xe.com
This website has a simple tool that allows you to find out the exchange rate for any two currencies.

Working abroad

Any Work Anywhere

www.anyworkanywhere.com
An easy-to-use site that allows you to search by location and job type to find a number of different programmes and recruiters worldwide.

Childcare International

www.childint.co.uk
An international agency that finds work for qualified childcare professionals. It offers a list of vacancies and details of what is required from you.

Crown Recruitment

www.workonship.co.uk
shipjob@aol.com

This recruitment agency supplies a wide variety of staff for Royal Caribbean and Carnival, two of the world's largest cruise lines.

Jobs Abroad

www.jobsabroad.com
A comprehensive search engine providing hundreds of links to jobs and recruitment companies around the world.

Monster

www.monster.com
A good place to look for more permanent jobs and career opportunities in Europe and America.

Seasonal work

Camp America

www.campamerica.co.uk
Tel: 0207 581 7373
A detailed and straightforward website that lays out what to expect from signing up to work on American summer camps.

Ski Staff

www.skistaff.co.uk
jobs@skistaff.co.uk
If you are looking for a winter season job then this is the website to visit. It has details on job vacancies and links to specialist companies.

Teaching English

British Council

www.britishcouncil.org/teacherrecruitment.htm

The British council offers opportunities for teaching English abroad and also gives advice on how to gain a TEFL qualification.

Dave's ESL cafe

www.eslcafe.com
This website is a great hub of information for all things related to teaching abroad and has a jobs board and interactive forum.

Internships

Bunac

www.bunac.org
Tel: 0207 251 3472
A popular and long running gap year company that arranges a variety of jobs, work placements and volunteer programmes around the world.

Mountbatten Institute

www.mountbatten.org
Tel: 0845 370 3535
The Mountbatten Institute offers a renowned internship programme in New York, allowing students to spend a year working at top US companies.

Volunteering

MaDVeNturer

www.madventurer.com
Tel: 0845 121 1996
Madventurer offer a mix of volunteer work and adventure travel, all taking place in small groups with good in-country support.

Raleigh

www.raleighinternational.org
info@raleigh.org.uk
Tel: 0207 183 1270
Raleigh has been running challenging expeditions for 25 years, combining volunteer work, adventure travel and physical activity.

Travellers worldwide

www.travellersworldwide.com
Tel: 01903 502595
As well as an extensive list of volunteer opportunities, this site has contact details for language and cultural courses.

Volunteer abroad

www.volunteerabroad.com
A comprehensive site for searching for volunteer opportunities, run by the same people as www.jobsabroad.com.

Communication

Facebook

www.facebook.com
This social networking site allows you to create a personal profile, upload pictures and keep in touch with your friends.

Skype

www.skype.com
Visit this site to download the Skype software for free or to sign into an existing account and start making calls.

Word Press

www.wordpress.com
The quickest and easiest place to start a blog, Word Press is free, easy-to-use and will help you share your adventures with friends and family.

Health and safety

Foreign Office

www.fco.gov.uk
Tel: 020 7008 1500
The foreign office should be your first port of call for travel advice, information about countries that are unsafe to visit and recommended immunisations. You can also use it to find out about passports, visas and embassies in the countries you are visiting.

Insure My Trip

www.insuremytrip.com
A comparison website where you can search through the various different travel insurance providers to find one that is right for you.

Travel Doctor Site

www.traveldoctor.co.uk
A detailed resource for finding out what immunisations you will need for the various countries that you are visiting.

World Health Organisation

www.who.int
The World Health Organisation has detailed and up-to-date information on any health issues across the world.

Equipment

Blacks

www.blacks.co.uk
Tel: 0800 056 0127
A good value outdoor store where you can pick up all the basics that you will need for your trip.

Nomad Travel

www.nomadtravel.co.uk
An online travel and outdoor store that offers some good discounts and stocks many of the top brands.

Accommodation

Global Freeloaders

www.globalfreeloaders.com
Find a couch to sleep on for free anywhere in the world with this global portal that lets you search for people willing to invite you into their homes.

Hostels

www.hostels.com
A comprehensive collection of hostels with ratings from other travellers. This is the site to visit if you need to find a hostel anywhere in the world.

Youth Hostel Association

www.yha.org.uk/yha-overseas
Tel: 01629 592700
The YHA provides some useful information about international hostels and offers a card which gets you discounts abroad.

Visas and passports

Passports

www.passport.gov.uk/passport
Find out all you need to know about getting or renewing a passport from this government run website.

Project Visa

www.projectvisa.com
This website is a useful addition to your favourites as it has an easy search facility that takes you to visa requirements for countries across the world.

Guidebooks and further information

Lonely Planet

www.lonelyplanet.com
Well loved travel guides with a popular forum on their website to meet and get advice from fellow travellers.

Rough Guides

www.roughguides.com
These classic travel guides also have some interesting articles on the website.

Timeanddate.com

www.timeanddate.com
This is a simple but very useful website where you can type in a country and find out what time it is. Stops you from waking up your parents in the middle of the night!

TNT Magazine

www.tntmagazine.com
This free Australian magazine is a good place to start finding jobs or accommodation in the country.

Transitions Abroad

www.transitionsabroad.com
A long standing website and magazine that has a wealth of information about living, working and volunteering abroad.

Whatsonwhen

www.whatsonwhen.com
Want to know what's going on wherever you are in the world? This simple search facility will help you out whether you are looking for festivals, cultural events or something more offbeat.

Book List

A Year in Provence
By Peter Mayle, Penguin, London, 2000.

Down Under
By Bill Bryson, Black Swan, London, 2001.

In Patagonia
By Bruce Chatwin, Summit Books, London, 1977.

On the Road
By Jack Kerouac, Viking Press, New York, 1957.

Out of Africa
By Karen Blixen, Penguin, London, 1999.

Wild Swans: Three Daughters of China
By Jung Chang, HarperPerennial, London, 2004.

Need - 2 - Know

Available Titles Include ...

Allergies A Parent's Guide
ISBN 978-1-86144-064-8 £8.99

Autism A Parent's Guide
ISBN 978-1-86144-069-3 £8.99

Drugs A Parent's Guide
ISBN 978-1-86144-043-3 £8.99

Dyslexia and Other Learning Difficulties
A Parent's Guide ISBN 978-1-86144-042-6 £8.99

Bullying A Parent's Guide
ISBN 978-1-86144-044-0 £8.99

Epilepsy The Essential Guide
ISBN 978-1-86144-063-1 £8.99

Teenage Pregnancy The Essential Guide
ISBN 978-1-86144-046-4 £8.99

Gap Years The Essential Guide
ISBN 978-1-86144-079-2 £8.99

How to Pass Exams A Parent's Guide
ISBN 978-1-86144-047-1 £8.99

Child Obesity A Parent's Guide
ISBN 978-1-86144-049-5 £8.99

Applying to University The Essential Guide
ISBN 978-1-86144-052-5 £8.99

ADHD The Essential Guide
ISBN 978-1-86144-060-0 £8.99

Student Cookbook - Healthy Eating The Essential Guide
ISBN 978-1-86144-061-7 £8.99

Stress The Essential Guide
ISBN 978-1-86144-054-9 £8.99

Adoption and Fostering A Parent's Guide
ISBN 978-1-86144-056-3 £8.99

Special Educational Needs A Parent's Guide
ISBN 978-1-86144-057-0 £8.99

The Pill An Essential Guide
ISBN 978-1-86144-058-7 £8.99

University A Survival Guide
ISBN 978-1-86144-072-3 £8.99

Diabetes The Essential Guide
ISBN 978-1-86144-059-4 £8.99

View the full range at **www.need2knowbooks.co.uk**. To order our titles, call **01733 898103**, email **sales@n2kbooks.com** or visit the website.

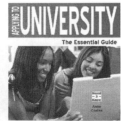
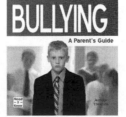
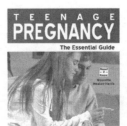

Need - 2 - Know, Remus House, Coltsfoot Drive, Peterborough, PE2 9JX